A SCHOOLBOY'S WAR IN SUSSEX

A SCHOOLBOY'S WAR IN SUSSEX

JAMES ROFFEY

Front cover: *The images of bomb damage and the RAF march have kindly been supplied by Littlehampton Museum.*

Frontispiece: *Pulborough carnival, 1931. (Garland Collection)*

First published 2010

The History Press
The Mill, Brimscombe Port
Stroud, Gloucestershire, GL5 2QG
www.thehistorypress.co.uk

British Library Cataloguing in Publication Data.
A catalogue record for this book is available from the British Library.

ISBN 978 0 7524 5518 1
Typesetting and origination by The History Press
Printed in Great Britain
Manufacturing managed by Jellyfish Print Solutions Ltd

DEDICATION

This book is dedicated to the people of Sussex who, during the dark years of the Second World War, did so much to ensure our country's ultimate victory. In addition to seeing their own young men and women leaving home to serve in the armed forces, they also saw the Battle of Britain being fought in the sky above their towns and villages.

They were on the front line of the expected enemy invasion, even to the extent of receiving government leaflets headed, 'What to do if the invader comes!' Their seaside towns and many villages became fortified zones, guarded by thousands of soldiers, many from Canada. Gun emplacements and machine-gun posts were built, and moveable tank barriers lined many of their roads, ready to use if the invasion came.

In addition to all that, the county was required to receive and care for thousands of children who had been evacuated from their families and homes in London and other places seen as being targets for enemy bombing. With few exceptions, the people of Sussex took the evacuees into their homes and often into their hearts.

As one of those evacuees, the most poignant memory I have of Sussex during the war comes flooding back to me whenever I hear that famous hymn 'Oh God our help in ages past, our hope for years to come'. As a small boy I sat in Pulborough Church on many Sunday mornings, alongside local people, Canadian soldiers and young men and women of all the services on leave. As we sang that hymn, we knew that local people of the Royal Observer Corps were on duty on the roof of the church tower high above us, keeping watch for enemy planes, parachutists or other signs of a possible invasion, just as their ancestors had done before them in earlier wars.

At wartime concerts held in the village hall we evacuees joined in the singing of 'Good old Sussex by the Sea' with great enthusiasm, which was often followed by 'There'll Always be an England and England Shall be Free'. In common with many thousands who, like me, were evacuated to Sussex, I will always be grateful to the people of that wonderful county.

James Roffey
July 2010

CONTENTS

1	Just Before the War	8
2	We're Off to the Country	13
3	I'll Take That One!	19
4	The 'Honeymoon' was Over	26
5	The Phoney War Period	35
6	We Shall Fight Them on the Beaches	42
7	Never in the Field of Human Conflict	58
8	Now Came the Bombers	66
9	The Highs and Lows of a Schoolboy's War in Sussex	70
10	School in a Hall and Other Places	80
11	Trains and Things That Went 'Clank' in the Night	85
12	Cup of Tea for Mr Whitehead	91
13	Ready to Do Battle	95
14	Days and Happenings that Make Memories	102
15	Let's Go to the Seaside!	113
16	Keeping in Touch with Home	119
17	You Can Come Home!	125

I

Just Before the War

No one really told me what was about to happen; perhaps because I was only eight years old they didn't think it was necessary, or that I wouldn't understand. I vaguely recall my father saying to me, 'It's nothing to worry about. It will be just like going on holiday and you will be home by Christmas.'

There was a lot of talk about another war. I heard about it on the wireless, as we then called it. When I was taken to the cinema we saw the newsreels and heard a man shouting in a foreign language; they said his name was Hitler, but I was more interested in the Mickey Mouse and Donald Duck cartoons. When the Wurlitzer organ rose up from below the stage I joined in singing the words shown on the screen.

My home was in a quiet, tree-lined road in Camberwell, South London, where the social rules were very strictly observed. I was the youngest of a family of five children – four boys and our sister. Every Sunday morning we boys wore our best suits and after being lined up for inspection by our father, who checked each of us to ensure that we had washed properly, that our hair was brushed, combed and plastered down with Brylcream and our shoes had been cleaned and polished, we were sent out to walk sedately around one of the several parks nearby. No ball games were allowed on Sundays, the swings, slides and roundabouts were chained up and padlocked, and the uniformed park keepers watched to see that we obeyed the 'Keep off the grass' signs. We walked quietly around the formal gardens, stopping to smell the scent of the roses and the lavender bushes. At the lake we would feed the ducks with the bread crusts we had brought for them. If it was a hot day we stopped at the ornate Victorian fountain to drink water from the iron cups that hung on chains.

Then it was time to go home to follow another strictly observed tradition, that of the family Sunday dinner (lunch) of roast beef, Yorkshire pudding, roast potatoes and greens according to the time of the year (I hated the Brussel sprouts, but had to eat every one that was put on my plate).

In the afternoon we went to Sunday school. The nearest church to our house was actually a Baptist chapel, but no main roads had to be crossed by us to reach it. The Sunday school was held in a nearby hall; the things I remember from that was all the children singing 'All things bright and beautiful' and of carefully sticking an 'attendance' stamp in a little booklet to ensure that we qualified to be taken on the annual summer outing to the seaside, but my worst memory was of being violently sick at a Christmas party! I never managed to get enough 'attendance' stamps in my booklet before the war brought an end to such outings.

Very little happened to disrupt the well-ordered routine of our lives but when the barrage balloons appeared in the sky over London and sandbags were stacked up in front of the Town Hall, the police and fire brigade stations, even I began to realise that 'something' was going to happen.

One Saturday afternoon with my brother John, who was only a year and a month older than me, I was sent on an errand to Camberwell Green, only about half a mile away. On the way we heard the sound of a band and soon we saw lots of men wearing black shirts marching to the thump, thump, thump of the drums and carrying banners. They turned off the main road and stopped in a cul-de-sac, where a man started to give a speech, but then a lot of shouting and fighting started and bricks were being thrown. Mounted policemen came and rode their horses straight into the crowd, striking out with their long batons. When we saw men lying in the road, streaming with blood, John and I ran home as fast as we could. 'Where have you been?' demanded our father. When we told him what we had seen he became very angry. 'Don't you know that the man was Oswald Mosley and the men in black shirts were all fascists!' he shouted. 'You must never go anywhere near them!' I didn't really understand what all the fuss was about.

The year was 1938 and many more strange things started to happen. One day when I arrived home from school I saw sheets of corrugated steel stacked outside every house, including ours. They had been delivered by the council and were to be used to erect what they called Anderson shelters. The following weekend my father and eldest brothers dug a deep hole in the back garden in which to construct the shelter. It was only a small back garden and the shelter took up most of the limited space. Our mother was not at all pleased to see the flowering plants she had carefully looked after all dug up, and she was also concerned about where she would now be able to hang out the washing every Monday.

The shelters were each provided with bunk beds, but when our mother saw them she was not at all impressed, 'If they think I am going to spend nights in that hole in the ground they've got another think coming!' she said. She became even more sceptical when the shelter began to fill with water after the first shower of rain.

It was of much greater fun for me when they issued us all with gas masks. That happened at school, where we had to learn the correct way in which to put them on and take them off. We were given strict lectures about how important they were and that we must carry them with us wherever we went. 'If there is a gas attack you will only have a few minutes in which to put your mask on!' they said. They were horrible, smelly things, but we boys soon discovered that it was easy to make very rude noises when wearing them, simply by breathing out hard. As the teachers could not see our faces with the masks on they had no way of knowing who had made the noise.

Then came the instructions to everyone to stick strips of brown paper across all the windows; that was to stop the glass splintering if a bomb dropped nearby. After that stirrup pumps were issued and householders were told to always have buckets of sand and water to hand in case incendiary bombs were dropped.

Increasingly I heard the word 'evacuation' being said at school, by my parents and on the wireless, but I didn't fully understand exactly what it meant. Then one day at school we were all given letters to take home. Each letter was in a brown envelope with the words, 'From His Majesty's Government. Urgent' printed on the front. 'Take this letter home and give it immediately to your parents! Don't lose it or get it dirty. It is very important!' said the teachers, all looking very serious and worried. I did as I was told and so did my sister Jean and our brothers John and Ernest. Our mother put them all unopened beside the clock on the high mantelpiece for when our father arrived home from work. As he opened them he became very angry, 'It's all starting again!' he shouted, 'They told us we were fighting the war to end all wars!' He had been a soldier in the First World War and had been gassed and injured. 'They will have to go,' he added. I didn't know what he meant, but our mother rushed out to the kitchen and we could hear saucepans and plates being banged about, which was a sure sign that she was very upset and probably crying.

Soon after that our parents attended a big meeting at my sister's school, where they were told all about the government's evacuation plans. Later they told me that if we were evacuated, John and I would go with Jean and her school, so that she could look after us. Brother Ernest would go with his school. It was then that my father told me, 'You have nothing to worry about and it will be just like going on holiday.'

Several months drifted by with nothing much happening that I was aware of. The schools broke up for the 1939 summer holidays but, like most people, we didn't go away. Then, halfway through the holidays, notices were issued recalling all the London schools and those in the other evacuation areas. Parents were told to send their children to the school they were registered to go away with. Everything was made ready for us all to leave as soon as the government issued the order to 'Evacuate Forthwith!' To me it was all quite exciting because I still didn't really understand what it was all about.

2

WE'RE OFF TO THE COUNTRY

I often think I may have been the only one who didn't realise it was evacuation day. The morning started very much as it had for several preceding ones, except I did notice that our mother seemed to be acting in a more 'matter of fact' way than was normal, even for her. She kept checking our little suitcases containing the things we were to take with us according to the lists that had been issued by the school, making sure that we had everything. She gave my shoes an extra rub with the polishing cloth and checked several times that I had brushed my teeth.

My brother John and I were repeatedly told that our sister Jean was in charge and that we were to do exactly what she said, with no arguing. The three of us set off to walk to our sister's school, carrying our gas masks, raincoats and suitcases, just as we had on several previous days. Mum did not walk with us as she was still seeing brother Ernie off to his school with his evacuation things.

When we arrived at the school I wondered why so many of the parents were standing outside the school gates and lining the pavements. Within minutes the teachers were blowing their whistles, which was the signal for us all to form up into a long 'crocodile' file that wound right around the playground. We had practised doing that many times during the previous days. But then something different happened; the teachers came round tying 'luggage' labels on to each one of us. The girls wore theirs on string hanging round their necks, while we boys had ours tied through the buttonhole of our jackets. I looked at my label, and all it had written on it was my name, that of the school and the words 'London County Council'. There was also the school party number, but I can't remember what that was.

A very tall policeman then arrived and the gates of the school playground were opened wide and, led by the policeman, we set off. Someone told me we were going to the nearest railway station, which I knew was called Peckham Rye, but instead of turning right to go along Rye Lane we carried straight on. There were lots of other policemen around and they were making all the mothers and others stay on the opposite side of the road; they were not allowed to walk with us or come near.

To me it was all very exciting. I saw it all as being part of a big adventure and couldn't understand why so many of the women and older girls were crying. I caught a glimpse of our mother in the crowd and waved to her, but she didn't wave back, I suppose she couldn't see me. Eventually we arrived at Queens Road Peckham Railway Station, where a line of policemen stood across the entrance. There was a scuffle as we went in because some of the mothers fought their way through the police cordon to snatch their children back. I couldn't understand why.

The railway lines at Queens Road are high above the road on an embankment and to reach the station platforms you had to climb up a steep flight of stairs. One of the girls tripped and fell, causing several others to also fall, but it all sorted itself out and no one was hurt. Once up on the platform we found that hundreds of other children from another school were already there. My memory of that part of the day was of teachers, railway staff and helpers repeatedly shouting at us to 'Move back! Move back!' but there was no room left to do that. I suppose they were afraid that some of us would fall off the platform onto the railway line.

It was already turning into a very hot day, my little suitcase seemed to get ever heavier, the string of my gas-mask box was cutting into my neck and it seemed as though we were going to remain on that crowded platform forever. Eventually a train made up of very dirty, old-fashioned carriages inched its way slowly into the station and alongside our platform. As soon as it stopped, a mad scramble began as the children struggled to get aboard. Each carriage was divided into little compartments that had a bench seat on each side. There were no corridors and therefore no toilets, the absence of which would create great problems for many of the children as the day wore on.

School friends, brothers and sisters pushed and shoved as they desperately tried to keep together. Our sister Jean somehow managed to keep hold of John and me and to get the three of us into the same little compartment; I even got a seat next to a window. There was another long wait before the last doors were slammed shut and the porters blew their whistles for the train to move off. We still had no idea where we were being taken; that was still a closely guarded secret.

Because there was no teacher or adult helper in our compartment to stop them most of the children immediately unpacked the food their mothers had given them, which was supposed to last for the rest of the day. Some had bottles of lemonade or Tizer, others had sticky cakes, bars of chocolate and packets of sweets. It was very hot on the train and very crowded. Some of the children had never travelled anywhere before and the results were inevitable – but there were no toilets! It all became very unpleasant in those little compartments!

The train trundled on relentlessly, not stopping at any stations, but several times it came to a jolting standstill in a siding. Once it started moving backwards and we all cheered because we thought 'they' had changed their minds and were taking us home. Our hopes were dashed when the train again moved forward and rapidly picked up speed. From my window seat I watched the changing scene – the rows of densely built terrace houses began to give way to the fairly new, semi-detached ones of the outer suburbs, each with their neatly manicured front and back gardens. Then I saw green fields with their surrounding hedges, and some had sheep or cattle grazing in them. 'Look!' I said, 'The buses are painted green, not red!'

Our train raced through many stations without stopping or even slowing down. Many years later I learnt that the signalmen had been instructed to ensure that all the signals were set at green for the evacuation trains and the drivers given strict orders not to stop at any station until their train reached its destination. Of course, we still didn't know where that was to be or what it was called. The houses became fewer and I saw farm buildings and haystacks. In some of the fields people were working; little did I know that soon I would also be helping with haymaking and harvesting.

Quite unexpectedly our train began to slow down as it approached a station and then came to a standstill. Immediately railwaymen came running along the platform, opening the doors of the little compartments. Soon hordes of children stepped out into the bright sunshine. Then all the shouting started again as teachers, helpers and porters hurried us out of the station, but first we had to line up at the W.H. Smith's bookstall to be given a carrier bag containing tins of food. We had no time to see exactly what we had been given.

Once we were out of the station the teachers tried to form us into rows, but there were so many of us crowded into a limited space that they soon gave up. Because there had been no toilets on the train, temporary ones had been set up in front of the station. They simply comprised a wooden frame over which sheets of canvas had been spread, but they only covered the tops and the backs, leaving the fronts wide open. Inside were wooden seats and beneath each was a shiny, galvanised iron bucket. I remember my sister saying, 'I may be busting to go, but I'm not using one of those with everyone gawping at me!' She had probably seen the row of village boys sitting on a nearby fence, waiting to see all those 'townee kids from Lundan'.

There were hundreds of children milling around the forecourt of that country station. Adults wearing various armbands were trying to check their lists and shout orders at us. Some of the older boys decided that they had had enough of being evacuees and when one of them spotted a road sign saying 'London 52 miles', they set off to walk home, but a policeman soon brought them back.

To avoid more of us wandering off, the adults decided to herd us all into the pens of the adjoining cattle market. We were all thirsty and had been travelling for hours, so a long queue soon formed at the only water tap. We were told that the reason we were being kept outside the railway station was because a fleet of double-decker buses should have been waiting to take us to the village school, but only one single-decker bus had actually arrived and that was shuttling between the station and the school, which was about a mile away. As there were hundreds of us, some had to wait a very long time.

Eventually it was our turn to scramble on to the bus, each carrying our little suitcases, gas masks, etc., and that new addition, the carrier bag containing tins of food. Waiting for us outside the school was a new ordeal – the so-called medical examination. Sitting on a wooden chair was a very fierce-looking (at least to me) woman. Beside her was a bucket containing strong-smelling disinfectant water that had a greenish look. Clutched in her hand she had a metal comb. We were made to form a single column in front of her and she immediately grabbed the first child in the column and, after dunking the comb in the disinfectant water, yanked it through the child's hair. Most of the boys had been given short haircuts just before evacuation day, which meant they soon had smelly disinfectant trickling down their necks.

After the torture with the comb and disinfectant the woman yanked our shirts up, I suppose to see if we had signs of measles or chicken pox. Then she poked a stick in our mouths; I thought she was trying to make us all sick, but someone said she was the local nurse and she was checking to see if we had a throat infection. After escaping from the fierce woman we were allowed to go into the tiny school, where waiting for us was a sight that should have cheered us up considerably. Down one side of the classroom were trestle tables piled high with sandwiches, cakes and biscuits. There were jugs of lemonade and big teapots filled ready with hot tea, beside bowls filled with sugar, jugs of milk and rows of cups and saucers. I was later told that the local women had been working since early that morning to prepare the refreshments for us as soon as they were given the message, 'The evacuees are on their way!' Some of them had been baking cakes for several days previously.

They were expecting us to rush to the tables excitedly, as children normally do; instead we all sat quietly on the bare wooden floor, waiting to see what was going to happen next. In fact, I don't think any of the children touched those lovely refreshments. I know I certainly didn't. By then all the excitement of setting off on what we had seen as being a great adventure had worn off. Apprehension had set in; we all wanted to go home. Some of the children were crying. 'Where are we?' we wondered. We all wanted to see our Mum, but she wasn't there.

'So this is evacuation!' I thought. 'A long journey in a crowded train, followed by ages spent in the pens of a cattle market. The smell of the disinfectant that has trickled down my neck. Now a feeling of anxiety as we all sit on the bare floorboards of a school in a place the name of which I still didn't know.' I didn't like evacuation anymore; I just wanted to go home.

3

I'll Take That One!

For quite a while, as we sat on the floor of Pulborough Village School, nothing much seemed to be happening apart from one or two important-looking men and women coming into the classroom, one of which wore a red armband that had printed on it in black letters 'BILLETING OFFICER'. Then a group of men and women came in and stood in front gazing at us. After the man wearing the Billeting Officer armband had finished talking to them, the men and women began pointing at certain children, saying, 'I'll take that one,' or 'Those two girls can come with me.'

Gradually most of the children were taken away, leaving just a few of us still sitting on the floor. The Billeting Officer was obviously getting worried. My brother and I were still sitting with our sister, who was keeping a tight hold of both of us, determined to carry out our parents' order not to allow us to be separated. 'Which boy would like to live on a farm?' shouted the Billeting Officer. My brother put his hand up, only to have it yanked down by our sister. Still more of the children were led away, but it seemed that no one could be found to take us three. Then the Billeting Officer came over and forcibly dragged John away, ignoring Jean's tearful attempts to stop him.

John had gone, no one would tell us where and Jean was in floods of tears. Then a young man told us we were both to go with him to his car that was parked on the road in front of the school. As soon as we were both safely in the back of the car he started the engine and off we went, travelling for mile after mile out of the village. I hoped that he was taking us home, but no such luck. He seemed quite friendly so I asked him where we were. Rather surprised that we did not know, he said, 'You are in Pulborough, West Sussex, and I am taking you to your billet.'

Eventually he turned off the main road to drive slowly along a very bumpy track. After a while he turned the car off the track, went through a gateway and stopped in front of a very dilapidated cottage. Its garden was overgrown with stinging nettles reaching right to the door. 'Get out of the car and come with me,' he said, and strode to the door of the cottage, upon which he knocked loudly. No one appeared and the door remained tightly closed, so he knocked again, much louder this time. Suddenly the door opened and a very cross-looking woman appeared. Her hair was tied up and covered by a headscarf, and she wore a wrap-round overall of the sort that many housewives used to wear in those days.

'Who are you and what do you want?' she shouted. The young man, who was obviously taken aback, replied, 'I have been sent by the Billeting Officer to bring these two evacuees.' She immediately answered, 'Well you can take them away again, I won't have any bloody evacuees!' and slammed the door shut. He knocked on the door again and the woman immediately opened it and again started shouting at him, but this time he put his foot in the doorway to stop her shutting it. Then he pushed us inside, saying, 'You've got to take them in by law; if you don't I'll call the police.' Although I didn't know it at the time, I learnt later that billeting was compulsory and that any householder in a reception area who refused to take in evacuees could be prosecuted if the local council could prove that they did have enough room.

Without saying another word the young man ran to his car and drove away. The woman was incandescent, 'You can't stay here!' she kept shouting at us, 'I have no spare room, or enough food in the house to feed you and the nearest shop is miles away.' Jean was in floods of tears. To try and help I gave the woman my carrier bag containing the tins of food that had been handed to me at the railway station. She looked inside and seemed slightly mollified, but she would have been less pleased if she had known that I had previously taken out the big bar of chocolate that was included. Jean also handed over her carrier bag, but she had left in her bar of chocolate and never saw it again.

By then the woman had let us into the kitchen of the cottage, where I wondered what the peculiar smell was. I soon found out that it was the smell of the oil lamps that were used for lighting. The cottage had no supply of gas, electricity or piped water. Quite near the back door was a well from which they got their water. I had seen pictures of country cottages that had wells with pretty tops and a hand-turned winch to wind up the buckets full of water, but this well had no such refinements. It was simply a deep, brick-lined hole in the ground, beside which was a battered metal bucket with a length of rope tied to its handle.

The woman was still furious at having had two evacuees dumped upon her. 'You can't stay here!' she kept shouting. 'I only have two bedrooms and what will HE have to say when he finds out?' I wondered a lot about who 'HE' could be and what he was really like. I imagined him to be a big, angry man who would shout at us even louder than the woman had, and probably throw us out.

'You two will have to sleep in my daughter's bedroom and she will have to share mine,' the woman said. 'But you will have to go first thing in the morning!' Poor Jean was still crying when later that evening she and I were shown up a steep flight of stairs, by the light of a flickering candle, to the daughter's bedroom. There was only a narrow, single bed for us both to sleep in. I tried hard to stop Jean from crying by forcing pieces of my chocolate into her mouth, but without success as she was so distraught.

The woman's daughter was quite nice to us when she arrived home from work and even managed to calm her mother down and made her realise that we couldn't be simply told to leave in the morning, although they were both concerned about what HE would have to say about us being there. Several days passed without any sign of the apparently all powerful HE. Meanwhile, I was given the job of drawing water from the well. 'Hold on tightly to the rope,' they said. 'Don't let go of it whatever you do, because it and the bucket will be lost down the well!'

Each bucket of water that came up had various insects swimming around and bits of grass and leaves floating about. 'Drink a glass of that water every morning,' they said, 'and you will never be ill!' Another of my jobs was to clean everyone's shoes. I had to sit outside the back door with a pile of them and all sorts of cleaning materials, but at home I had never even cleaned my own shoes (my mother always did that) so I was not very good at it.

I gradually found out that the mysterious HE owned the cottage but lived and worked in London, only coming down to spend the occasional weekend in Sussex. I also discovered that there were other, better-furnished rooms in the cottage which Jean and I were forbidden to enter, although we did manage to see into some of them through their ground-floor windows.

One morning a large car arrived and HE got out and strode into the cottage. The normally fierce woman immediately became all smiles and softly spoken as she hurriedly made him some coffee. 'I'm afraid we have had two evacuees billeted upon us,' she said. 'I told the man who brought them that they couldn't stay here, but he refused to listen,' she added.

HE apparently told her to bring us into his sitting room, and I expected him to start shouting, but instead he was very friendly and made us welcome. When Jean told him how John had been dragged away from her and we had no idea where he was, he immediately said, 'I'll sort that out!' and set off in his car to the main village. About an hour later he returned, with John sitting in the car. 'Here he is!' said the man. 'He is billeted on a farm and is being very well cared for. I'll take him back this evening after tea.' How he had found him we will never know. I suppose he knew the Billeting Officer.

During the afternoon he took us to visit his friends who lived nearby in a large house which had a lake in its grounds. It was there that I had my first experience of being treated as if I was an alien object. The people who lived there had a young daughter who took us rowing on the lake, which I thought was wonderful. Later she thought she would take us into the house, but before she could do so her mother stopped her, saying, 'Where are you taking them, darling?' The daughter replied, 'Oh I'm taking them to meet Daddy, is he in the study?' Looking shocked, her mother said, 'Oh darling, you shouldn't do that! I am sure your little friends are very nice, but they are only evacuees so we don't really want them in the house, do we! I'll have some barley water and buns sent out for them on a tray,' she added.

Being older that me, Jean was fully aware of the condescension that had been shown. 'She can keep her barley water and buns!' she muttered. Very soon after HE took us back to the cottage where, much to her disgust, the woman was told to serve us tea in one of his private rooms. Then he took John back to his billet and returned to London. We never saw him again and immediately after he left the woman reverted to her bad-tempered ways.

A few days later the Billeting Officer arrived to take us to new billets in the main village. Jean was billeted with the family of a railway signalman and I, to my great delight, was taken to live in a sweet shop. Later that day John was also brought to live there, which came as a surprise to our foster parents as they had told the Billeting Officer that they could only take one girl evacuee in an emergency.

It was a typical country shop of those times that sold groceries, tobacco, fresh vegetables, cups of tea and, for a few coppers, stored the bicycles of people who had ridden to the nearby railway station to catch a train. The shop was actually in what had been the front room of a semi-detached house. Behind it was the family's living room, which also served as where the many cups of tea and light snacks were prepared. Upstairs were the bedrooms.

I think that when I was taken into the shop by the Billeting Officer I must have been eyeing the display of sweets and chocolate too intensely, because my foster father put on a stern look and said, 'You must never help yourself, but if you are a good boy and willingly do all the jobs we set you, we will give you a pennyworth of sweets every day and two pennyworth on Sundays.' In those days a penny would buy ten toffees and two pennies would buy a bar of chocolate.

That seemed a wonderful arrangement to me, so I kept my side of the bargain. The jobs I were given included filling and carrying in the buckets of coal needed for the kitchen range, chopping firewood, feeding the chickens, cleaning out the hen houses, collecting the eggs and, much harder, carrying the very heavy full cans of water from the house up to the hen houses. My foster father also had several allotments where he grew all our vegetables, and I was expected to help.

Throughout the first few weeks after our arrival at Pulborough there was no schooling, although the head teacher of Jean's school was making every effort to find premises in which classes could be held. It was thought that the old Corn Exchange could be suitable, but it hadn't been used for several years and was in a poor condition. Its use as a corn exchange had ceased many years ago, but as the then biggest 'hall' in the village it had served as the main venue for local events, such as dances, whist drives, public meetings and other such functions, many of them being held to raise the funds to build a new village hall.

Eventually that was achieved, the new village hall was built and the opening ceremonies held, leaving the old Corn Exchange locked up and disused. It actually belonged to the rambling old Swan Hotel, which through the ages had been a prosperous coaching inn on the main road from London to the south coast. Now known as the A29, that road is on the line of the Roman Stane Street. Hanging in the Corn Exchange was a large painting of the Laughing Cavalier, and it was said that he had looked down upon many events held there over the years, from society weddings to celebrations of the end of the Boer War, the First World War and innumerable other occasions.

During the years of disuse, the old Corn Exchange became very shabby and run down. Thick dust coated its floor and whatever furniture had been left there. The Laughing Cavalier still hung on the far wall, but there were no crowds of people or bands playing to keep him smiling. However, the idea of using it as a school for the evacuees seemed to be the solution to a major problem and the word was passed around the village that we evacuees were to report to the Corn Exchange one day to help get it ready. We all worked hard, sweeping up the thick dust, cleaning the walls and windows, and even the Laughing Cavalier was carefully dusted, but left in his time-honoured place.

We all thought that was where our school was to be held, but then it was discovered that the floor was unsafe; old floorboards and timber joists were crumbling away with dry rot and for safety reasons the old Corn Exchange could not be used. For a few more days we were free to enjoy the glorious late summer weather and, to me, evacuation really did seem to be 'just like being on holiday', as my father had promised. Then the order that we were to attend the village school was issued and reality set in.

4

THE 'HONEYMOON' WAS OVER

The first few weeks spent exploring and getting to know my way around Pulborough could be described as a honeymoon period. Every day the sun was shining, harvesting was in full swing, and time passed quickly as hours were spent leaning on the stone walls of the bridges over the River Arun, watching the shoals of fish swimming in the crystal-clear water.

That came to an abrupt end when my foster parents received notice that I and all the other evacuees were to start going to the village school. Attempts to find separate premises for the evacuees had so far come to nothing and somehow we all had to be crammed into the three classrooms of the St Mary's Church of England School.

It was then that we came face-to-face with the village boys, and what can only be described as all-out warfare began. Running fights between them and the evacuees became a daily occurrence. Initially the evacuees had the advantage because in addition to we boys who had been evacuated with our sisters' school, another large group from Leo Street School of Peckham had also been sent to Pulborough. Compared to the quiet part of Camberwell where my home was, Leo Street was in a 'tough' area of Peckham, adjacent to the famous Old Kent Road and nearer to the docklands.

Most of the Leo Street boys were older than me and could more than hold their own in any playground 'scuffles'. Sadly for us they did not stay in Pulborough for long; I think that most of them returned home to Peckham. That left the village boys in the supremacy and a favourite trick of theirs was to single out an evacuee boy and form a ring around him in the school playground, taunting and shouting at him until the teachers came running to stop them. Fortunately that never happened to me, but it did to my brother John.

Another idea of fun for them was to ambush an evacuee on his way to or from school. However, I became adept at avoiding them. After that came the craze for chalking messages on walls and buildings, saying, 'Vaccies go home. We don't want you here!' That was especially hurtful to us because all we wanted to do was to go home; homesickness had already become a problem, one that we would have to silently endure but never talk about because no one would understand. If we showed any sign of being unhappy we were quickly told to think ourselves lucky and stop being miserable.

The popular belief was that we evacuees from London missed the noise and bustle of town life, finding rural Sussex to be too quiet for us. In fact our great problem was that of wanting to be back in our real homes, with our families, where we belonged. Nowadays homesickness is recognised as being a psychological condition that can prove harmful if allowed to continue, but in the 1940s it was looked upon as a sign of weakness. Fortunately, as the weeks and months passed, the worst signs of resentment by the village boys abated and as the war developed we were all chalking up a new message, that of 'V for Victory'.

However, many latent problems remained and some of the people who had willingly taken evacuees into their homes during the early days of the war became less amenable as the months turned to years. Also, evacuees were no angels; like all children they misbehaved and got into trouble, although all too often they were wrongly blamed for field gates being left open resulting in cattle straying, and other such mishaps.

I was more fortunate than many evacuees because my foster father would stand up for me. Because the little shop where I was billeted became very busy, I was always sent out on long walks when not at school. With my brother John and Brian, another evacuee, we would walk for miles all around the village, but somehow always got back in time for meals, even though none of us possessed a watch.

One day when I returned from one of our walks of discovery, I realised that something was wrong. My foster father had got his stern face on and said, 'I want words with you, young man.' Then he said, 'Have you boys been to Park Farm today?' We hadn't and I told him so. Then he said, 'Are you telling the truth, because a woman from Park Farm has been here saying that all the chicken coops have been tipped over, rabbit hutches have been left open, hens' eggs smashed and all sorts of damage done and that she knows you boys are to blame!'

I insisted that we were not guilty and when the woman came again he told her she was wrong, saying, 'My evacuee is a good boy and I trust him. He looks after my chickens and he is not a liar.' The woman flew into a temper and accused him of covering up for me, shouting, 'He is only an evacuee and doesn't know any better!' His response was to send for the police, who later questioned me, and I heard nothing more about the trouble for several weeks, but then I was told that one of the farm workers' sons had owned up to the mischief. My foster father said it would be better if we never went to Park Farm again, which was a pity because it was one of our favourite places. In fact it was where John had been billeted during our first few weeks at Pulborough and he had been very happy there and well cared for. We had the free run of the farm and had watched with great interest everything that went on, such as the hand milking of the cows, seeing the piglets in their sties and the ferrets at work catching wild rabbits.

Of special interest was the great steam traction engine when it was fired up ready to run the threshing machines. The stooks of corn would be taken from the ricks and placed onto a conveyor belt leading to the threshing machine. Soon the grains of corn would be pouring into the waiting sacks, while the straw was carried away to be used for bedding the horses and other animals. Great clouds of steam would billow from the traction engine and occasionally shouts would come from the farm workers that a conveyor belt had slipped off its pulley or had broken.

However, the greatest excitement happened when the sheaves had been lifted from the rick down to the bottom layer. That was when all the men and every available boy formed a ring around the rick, all holding sticks, many with a straining, barking dog. They were there to kill as many as possible of the dozens of rats that would run out trying to escape. The little Jack Russell terrier dogs were the most fearless, rushing headlong into the rats, jaws snapping and flinging dying rats over their shoulders. Any rats that escaped the dogs would be clubbed by the men and boys. All that, of course, was before today's combine harvesters were invented.

Mondays were also exciting days at Pulborough throughout the war. They were market days, when the pens into which we were put when we first arrived were used for their real purpose. From early in the morning cattle trucks would arrive loaded with beasts to be sold by the auctioneers. Some carried young calves, others sheep, even bulls. As well as those brought by lorries, others arrived 'on the hoof', as the saying goes. They would be driven along the main roads by men with dogs. On market days everyone in the village took great care to see that their garden gates were closed and properly fastened. The saying amongst the country men was that, 'Only fools and townees leave their gates open on market days.'

The shop where I was billeted became very busy on market days; all the farmers and farm workers would crowd in for cups of tea and to buy their cigarettes, especially when the news could be heard on the wireless, which had to be turned up especially loud so that every word could be heard. Each bulletin would start with the announcer saying, 'This is the BBC Home Service. Here is the news read by...' and he would give his name, such as Bruce Belfrage or Alva Liddell. For a short while Wilfred Pickles was another of the news readers. No one spoke whilst the news was on. I followed it as keenly as anyone, partly because I needed to know how to position the little flags on my war maps, but more importantly due to my great desire for the war to end so that I could go home.

I became very well known to all the farmers and others who used to crowd into the little shop and I had to endure a lot of teasing. 'Our little smiler', they used to call me. Some would try to tickle me, but if anyone put their arm around my shoulders to give me an affectionate hug I would struggle free and run off. Why did I do that? It was because I was so affected by hidden homesickness I was afraid that any sign of affection would make me burst out crying, and that was something I must never do, because in those days it was drilled into us that 'Big boys don't cry!'

Across the doorway between the shop and the living room my foster father had constructed a big wooden screen with shelves, on which were placed big jars of sweets. As the war developed and confectionary was rationed and in short supply, many of the jars stood empty, which suited me because I could then see through into the shop. I spent quite a lot of time hiding behind those sweet jars and listening to what the people in the shop were saying. Many things happened during the war that were supposed to be secret, or at least not talked about in front of children, especially we evacuees.

Not everything that I heard from my hiding place behind the sweet jars was bad news; there was also a lot of humour. Market days were the best because that was when many farmers would gather in the shop to drink cups of tea. One day I heard them talking about the threat of invasion by German parachutists and a very elderly farmer, speaking in his broad Sussex accent, said, 'I keeps a loaded shotgun by me at all times and the first Gerry that lands on my farm gets both barrels!' All the others laughed and one said, 'Why you daft old fool, his mates will shoot you dead within minutes!' To which the elderly farmer replied, 'Well in that case I'll die 'appy, knowing as 'ow I've taken one of they buggers with me!'

The cattle market was a great attraction to me and when not at school I spent a lot of time there watching all that went on. Soon I was poking and prodding the sheep in the pens just like the farmers did, not that I really knew why they did that. As well as the farmers the auctioneers also used to come into the shop for their lunch. They all knew me and one day they decided on a big tease, in collusion with my foster father. During the auction of some sheep I had been there as usual, watching what went on and how the farmers would manage to bid without anyone knowing who it was, accept the auctioneer.

On the day of the big tease an auctioneer came into the shop and, keeping a straight face, asked me when I was going to pay for the sheep I had bid for. 'I haven't bid for any sheep!' I spluttered. 'Oh yes you have,' he replied, 'During the bidding you scratched your nose with your left hand. That means you were bidding and as no more bids were made yours was accepted and you must pay up and remove the sheep from the market!' 'But I haven't got any money!' I protested, to which he replied, 'That's your problem!' My foster father, who had been looking on, joined in the big tease, saying, 'I'm not paying for the sheep!' They kept up the pretence for quite a while before bursting into laughter, but what a scare they gave me, a nine-year-old boy.

Sometimes things would go wrong in the market, such as when bullocks panicked and broke free to go charging through the village, with farmhands and dogs trying to catch them. One day a bull with long horns charged his handlers and galloped straight through the main entrance of the nearby railway station. Some wag said, 'He's running to catch the next train!' But others were more worried, and justifiably so because the railway line there was electrified and if the bull had jumped off the platform he could have come into contact with the live line. Fortunately they managed to get him out of the station before that happened.

Evacuated children were not the only Londoners to be moved to Sussex during the early weeks of the war. The famous Max Factor cosmetic company decided to move one of their factories from London to the believed safety of West Sussex. At Pulborough they took over a large house called Templemead to use as a packing factory. The young women who worked there were housed in a large building called New Place Manor, which in spite of its name was actually very ancient.

The young women, however, found the village too quiet for their liking and soon began to drift back to London. This was not what Max Factor wanted and in an attempt to keep their staff from going home, they decided to hire the Corn Exchange for social events. Of course they soon found out that the floor was unsafe, just as Miss Ambler of the Peckham school had. Not to be beaten, Max Factor, a very wealthy company, paid to have a new sprung dance floor installed. When that was completed they booked several of the popular London bands to play for dancing on Saturday evenings, bringing the long-silent Corn Exchange back to life. But the young women from London were still leaving their jobs to go home. The dances failed because there were not enough young men left in the village to be dancing partners, most of them already having gone to join the armed forces.

The management of Max Factor gave up the struggle and moved their factory back to London. However, within a very short time the first of hundreds of Canadian soldiers arrived to set up camps in the area. From my hiding place behind the sweet jars at the shop I heard a lot of laughing and comments such as, 'Max Factor should have stayed a bit longer, the Canadians would have kept the girls happy!' I was too young to understand the full meaning of those comments.

The old Corn Exchange continued to be used for dances and social events, with the Laughing Cavalier still looking on from his place high on the wall above the bands. It was an integral part of the rambling old Swan Hotel, which was a former coaching inn on the main road between London and the south-coast towns of Littlehampton and Bognor Regis. Now known as the A29 it was originally the Roman Stane Street. Many years had passed since horse-drawn stage coaches had called at the Swan, their place being taken by motor coaches and cars, although that traffic had virtually ceased due to the war. The old Swan Hotel, however, became very busy indeed. In common with many country hotels, all its rooms

The Swan Hotel on Station Road. (Vine Collection)

were booked on a permanent basis by retired people who had evacuated themselves from London due to the threat of bombing.

The Swan was not the only hotel in Pulborough; it was in competition with the Railway Hotel, the Chequers, the Arun Hotel and the Spring Green Lady Guest House. In addition there were the several public houses, namely the Five Bells, Oddfellows and the Red Lion, with even more nearby. Although too young to know much about pubs, I was fascinated by the names of the brewery companies that then owned them, such as Ind Coope & Allsop, Friary Ales, Henty & Constable and Tamplins. All the breweries were located many miles from Pulborough and when petrol rationing began, beer deliveries became a problem. One day I was amazed to see a steam-powered lorry chugging through the village. Black smoke was belching from its chimney as its two-man crew struggled to steer it and keep it moving, albeit very slowly. Painted on its side were the words 'Henty & Constable, Chichester'.

Soon there were beer shortages and notices appeared in the pub windows saying 'NO BEER'. However, that rarely happened at the Swan Hotel and its bars were always crowded, especially with Canadian soldiers whose base had been set up just along the road in Templemead after Max Factor had left. The Swan belonged to Tamplins, whose brewery was in Brighton. Many Army lorries passed between Brighton and Pulborough, stopping if necessary to pick up barrels of beer for the Swan Hotel.

My brother John had been moved to another billet because our foster parents found they could not cope with looking after two evacuees as well as running the increasingly busy shop and tearooms. He was now living in a house next door to the Swan Hotel and from his bedroom window he could look into the Corn Exchange, listen to the bands and watch the dancing.

Throughout the duration of the war, the old Swan Hotel was a focal point for the thousands of soldiers in the area. It was also the base of the Home Guard and the fire brigade, and hosted various military exercises to test the effectiveness of the anti-invasion measures that were supposed to halt a German invasion force and stop it making further progress towards London, should a landing on the sandy beaches of Littlehampton have been achieved.

5

THE PHONEY WAR PERIOD

After the disruption of the arrival of thousands of evacuees into the towns and villages of Sussex and once the many problems of billeting had been at least temporarily resolved, things began to settle down. We had entered that period known as the Phoney War. The British Expeditionary Force was in France, the French Army was manning their believed-to-be impregnable Maginot Line and the popular song that we were all singing was 'We're going to hang out the washing on the Seigfried Line', that being the German defensive line built to rival its French counterpart.

On the face of things nothing much was happening in Britain; no enemy aircraft of any consequence were flying over the country and no bombs had fallen on London or any other town. The evacuation seemed to many people to be totally unnecessary and the drift home of evacuees which started as a trickle soon became a flood. Homesickness became a major problem for most of the evacuated children, resulting in many plaintive letters being secretly sent home to parents with the words, 'Please, please, let me come home, I am so very unhappy!' Parents, who were missing their children and wanted them back, quickly responded and many hundreds of evacuees left the reception areas.

Not all parents, however, were so receptive and ignored their children's pleas. Also, the authorities had instructed the foster parents to read the letters written by the evacuees in their care before they were posted and to not allow any that contained unsuitable wordings to be posted. Whilst that was understandable in many respects, it did have some unfortunate results. It is a sad fact that some evacuees were not being well looked after by their foster parents; some were not being properly fed, others were living in totally unsatisfactory conditions and, even worse, some were being sexually abused. Many evacuees had no money whatsoever and therefore were unable to purchase the necessary postage stamps.

A few parents had the foresight before the evacuation took place to hide a few stamped-addressed envelopes in their children's things that they were to take away with them. Some even gave their children secret code words that they were to use in their letters home if things were going wrong, such as the name of a cat or dog at home which did not actually exist. If a code word was used in a child's letter, their parents would immediately rush to the reception area and take them home.

A few of my evacuee friends decided to run away and make their own way home. They wanted me to join them, but I refused. Perhaps it was the thought of walking the fifty-two miles back to London, or maybe it was because I knew how angry my parents would have been if I had tried. In any case, although I was very homesick, I was being well cared for.

In those days it was quite easy to get on a train at most country stations without having bought a ticket, but at the main line stations there were manned barriers where you had to hand over your ticket to be allowed through. Many runaway evacuees were detected at the barriers and were held at the stations while the police contacted their parents, who had to come and collect them, also paying the missing train fare of course.

For the first few weeks of the evacuation parents were actively discouraged by the government from visiting their evacuated children. They were told it would unsettle us. However, after a while, that was either relaxed or ignored and various coach companies began to run 'visit the evacuees' specials. At Pulborough we were told that a fleet of coaches was coming from South London with our parents to visit us. They would arrive at the Swan Hotel the following Sunday morning. To me that meant immediately after breakfast, but Jean, our sister, knew that the coaches would not arrive at Pulborough until nearly midday, so the three of us went for a walk to one of our nearby favourite places. Its name was Old Place, where there were ancient barns and houses built of locally quarried stone and a placid lake dotted with water lilies and tall reeds. Elegant swans swam gracefully and there were many insects known as 'water boatmen' seemingly walking on the surface of the lake. It was, and still is, a magical place. The three of us sat on the low stone wall beside the water and Jean, who was always like a second mother to John and me, carefully checked to see that we had combed our hair and that our fingernails were clean. 'I won't have you showing me up to Mum,' she said. 'And another thing, don't you go upsetting Mum by saying you want to go home,' she added.

The hours passed oh-so-slowly as we waited for the coaches to arrive. We were among crowds of evacuees gathered outside the Swan Hotel, all eagerly waiting the arrival of our parents. Midday came and the big public bar that faced the road opened for business, but there were no refreshments for us children. Suddenly a cheer went up – the first coach had just come down Church Hill and was rounding the corner to pull on to the forecourt of the Swan. I know that there were several coaches in the convoy but I was too intent on looking for our Mum and Dad to bother about counting them.

I think Jean saw our parents first and we pushed our way through the crowd to get to them. Other parents were sweeping their children up in their arms, with lots of kisses and hugs, but our parents were not the demonstrative type, so we were not surprised when that didn't happen to us. Apparently one of the coaches had broken down on the way and another had taken a wrong turning, which was why they had arrived much later than expected. Several of the parents immediately went into the bar of the Swan, which made our mother very angry. 'They are treating this as if it was a works outing!' she said. Whether our father had ideas of 'wetting his whistle' I don't know, but if he did he knew better than to suggest it.

The five of us made our way along the road to where we were billeted. It had been arranged that we would all have lunch in the tearoom of the shop. But first we had to introduce our mother and father to our foster parents, and it was then that I first heard the words, 'Is he being a good boy?' used by my mother as they met my foster parents. I was to hear those words many times during the following four years. In fact, probably for the first time in my young life, I experienced a feeling of disillusionment.

My parents somehow seemed different to how I remembered them back at home. No doubt that visit was a great ordeal for them, but to me all they seemed concerned about was whether I was being a good boy.

All too soon it was time for us all to gather again outside the Swan, but this time it was to say goodbye when the coaches returned from picking up parents in other villages. When my parents stepped onto their coach it all became too much for me and I burst out crying. My mother's immediate response was to say, 'Now then, that's enough of that nonsense. Big boys don't cry!' But as the coach moved off I noticed that she was wiping her eyes with a handkerchief. Then they were off and the coaches rounded the corner to climb up Church Hill on the way back to London and the three of us walked disconsolately back to our billets. Another month was to pass before we saw our parents again. Generally the foster parents did not welcome the parental visits because they unsettled the evacuees and made them difficult to cope with, but as the war developed the visits became less frequent.

Not much happened during the next few months. The head teacher of the Peckham Central School for Girls finally managed to obtain the use of the village hall and all the girls went there every day for their lessons. Jean was moved to another billet at the other end of the village so John and I rarely saw her; in fact, her foster mother ordered us away when we tried to visit her and said we were not to call again; I don't know why.

The winter of 1939/40 was one of the coldest on record, making life very bleak. It was so cold the birds were dropping dead from the trees and John and I made a little graveyard for the ones that we found; it was under the fir trees that still stand in front of the railway station. One of my regular jobs was to go to the chicken runs and break the ice in their water bowls.

We evacuee boys had to attend the village school, which was ill-equipped to cope with such severe weather. The classrooms were bitterly cold, the water taps were frozen for weeks and the daily milk was even frozen when it arrived. In those days schoolboys were not allowed to wear long trousers until they were aged fourteen and ready to start work. As a result we all soon had chilblains and chapped legs, but no one seemed to care. The distance from my billet and the village school was about a mile and as I had to go back to the shop for lunch, that meant I did that walk four times a day, whatever the weather. Of course at that time there was no such thing as school dinners.

Life for we evacuees at the village school was not a very happy experience. As I have mentioned before, there was often friction between us and the village boys, but to be fair there were faults on both sides. They would shout, 'Go home, you dirty Londoners!', to which we would reply, 'Get back in your pig sties, you country bumpkins!' Unfortunately some of the teachers were not too well disposed towards the evacuees. Part of the problem was that, educationally, some London schools were ahead of those in the rural areas; therefore that gave us an advantage when questions were asked, because we had already learnt about the relevant subject and knew the answers. It must have been difficult for a teacher to constantly see the evacuees' hands go up first in response to many of the questions. It was also resented by the local children, but that wasn't our fault.

The village school did not have a proper playground, just an area of wasteland at the back which used to be a sand quarry. Part of it was covered with prickly gorse bushes in which 'secret' dens were set up. One of them 'belonged' to an older village boy who had nearly reached school-leaving age. Although I was totally naïve about such things, I instinctively knew that it was wrong for him to encourage younger boys to go into his den and then persuade them to drop their trousers so that he could 'just have a look'. I always kept well away from him. Then he seemed to disappear and my foster father asked me if I knew him. I replied saying that I thought he was weird and never spoke to him. I was told that he had gone away to live in a school for Army cadets, but I wonder what the true story was.

As John's new billet was just along the road from the shop I saw him virtually every day and was always made welcome by his foster mother. It was nice to go into a house that was not dominated by the demands of a shop. My foster parents had two grown-up children; their son Leonard was serving in the Royal Navy and the room I slept in was really his bedroom. I was told not to touch any of his books or other things. During his occasional leaves he would stay with his parents and sometimes take John and me rowing on the River Arun, having hired one of the little fleet of boats from the boatyard near the Swan Hotel, which belonged to the appropriately named Mr and Mrs Float.

Gwen, the daughter of my foster parents, worked in the shop. She had not long since left school when we evacuees arrived and immediately became my close friend. She took John and me on exploration walks around the village and along the remote country lanes, taking care to explain to us which of the wild plants were poisonous, where the best blackberries could be found and how to tell the difference between mushrooms and toadstools. She would also take us fishing in the river. At first I only had a homemade fishing rod, but she persuaded her parents to let me use one of Leonard's that was kept in the garden shed. I am still in touch with Gwen and visit her when I can.

Although the shop was open until 8 p.m. every day, it was not busy then and I used to spend hours with Gwen, sitting on a stool behind the counter. As the war developed and items such as cigarettes became in short supply, I was sworn to secrecy about what was stored on the shelves under the counter. Like all shopkeepers at that time, my foster father tried to look after his regular customers in preference to others. Increasingly many of them were Canadian soldiers who could get plenty of cigarettes and chocolate from their NAAFI shop.

In May 1940 Germany invaded Holland and Belgium, then France. The British Army was driven back to the coast at Dunkirk, to be rescued by the Royal Navy and the famous fleet of small boats. Many trains passed through Pulborough Station in which we saw soldiers with bloodstained bandages and torn uniforms. Winston Churchill became Prime Minister; France surrendered. The Battle of Britain, much of which would be fought in the skies above Sussex, would soon begin. The Phoney War was over.

6

WE SHALL FIGHT THEM ON THE BEACHES

We shall fight them on the beaches...
We shall fight in the fields and streets...
We shall never surrender.

It is sometimes said that British schoolboys are the most patriotic of anyone. They certainly were during the Second World War, especially if they were evacuees. I clearly remember the scene in my foster father's shop when Winston Churchill's words boomed out from the wireless. The shop was crowded to capacity with people; they included porters from the railway station, and drivers and conductors from the Southdown buses that stopped for a short while outside, waiting to connect with the trains. Portable radios were not then available. While Churchill was speaking everyone stood in total silence, but when he finished they all cheered and clapped. I could see and hear everything from my place behind the sweet jars.

Evidence of people's determination to fight was everywhere to be seen. News of the German parachutists landing in Belgium caused Sussex farmers with large, open fields that could have made ideal landing areas for enemy gliders to drag out a wide variety of obstacles, such as disused farm carts, old cultivators and drilling machines – even empty oil drums were placed in the fields. Later the Army set up timber posts with connecting wires that would have wrecked any gliders trying to land.

Thousands of Canadian soldiers came and set up camps, where their vehicles, guns and tents were all covered with camouflage netting. Tanks, bren gun carriers and Army lorries clogged the narrow streets of the villages and all the connecting lanes. Big concrete gun emplacements were hastily built at carefully chosen locations, from where advancing enemy tanks could have been blown to pieces. Both of the bridges over the River Arun, near the Swan Hotel, had holes driven into their road surfaces into which steel barriers could be fitted to prevent tanks and other vehicles being driven over. It was rumoured that both the road and the railway bridge had been mined, ready to be blown up if necessary.

Behind the stone walls around Swan Corner, machine-gun posts were built, each with slits through which our soldiers could fire. The steep hill leading up to the church was honeycombed with slit trenches and more machine-gun posts. At the top of the hill was another big gun emplacement, from which there was a clear view of the main road leading from the coast. Had the enemy come they would have been met by a barrage of shells, machine-gun bullets and soldiers ready with rifles to pick off any foot soldiers.

Also standing proudly at the top of the hill was the ancient parish church with its tower, from the top of which was a clear, panoramic view of the surrounding countryside, especially to the south, from which an invading army was expected to come at any time. On the top of the tower an observation post was set up, from which warning signals could be sent to our troops. Great coils of barbed wire were set up around that part of the village. They ran through people's gardens and across fields. Their presence caused a problem to the occupants of the house next to where John was billeted, because the wire ran across the path leading to their outside lavatory. After protests, a way through was made for them.

The reason for all those anti-invasion measures was that Pulborough was on what the Army called a 'stop line'. If the Germans had landed on the sandy beaches of the south coast beside the seaside town of Littlehampton and managed to break out from their beachhead, they were expected to make a Panzer drive towards London. But once over the South Downs they would have needed to cross the marshy lands through which the River Arun meandered, known as the Brooks. A key road was the A29, leading straight to Pulborough.

It therefore became a fortified village and was subject to high-security measures. Anyone entering or leaving the village was liable to be stopped by the police or the Army and required to prove their identity. If you lived in the village all you needed to show was your identity card. The number on mine was ENAK 81/5. I believe that ENAK was the code for Pulborough, 81 denoted which house or cottage I lived in and 5 was my individual number. The way that worked was simple – No. 1 was my foster father, 2 my foster mother, 3 was Gwen their daughter, 4 was my brother John (he was still billeted there when the identity cards were issued), and I was 5.

Anyone visiting Pulborough had to have a special permit, so if my mother was visiting I had to go to the police station to get one for her. My father could rarely visit because he was working seven days a week in the London Docks, as well as serving in the Home Guard.

It is rather surprising that we evacuees were not moved from Pulborough during the threatened invasion, because many places all along the south and east coasts had their status changed from that of 'Reception' to 'Evacuation'. This meant that children who had been evacuated to places such as Brighton, Worthing, Shoreham, Bognor Regis and others along the south coast, and others taken to Lowestoft, Great Yarmouth and places along the east coast, were all re-evacuated, together with the local children.

I believe that a twelve- or thirteen-mile-deep belt from the coast was affected, but Pulborough was just beyond that and therefore not evacuated, even though it had become a major defensive site. The next village south of Pulborough, named Coldwaltham, was evacuated.

Every household in Pulborough was issued with a government leaflet entitled, 'What To Do If The Invader Comes!' Briefly it told people to 'Stay Put' and not try to move away. That was because they didn't want the roads to become clogged with people trying to move north, away from the invading German Army. In France, Belgium and Holland that had happened and the roads became so clogged the defending army could not get its reinforcements through. Also the German Air Force had machine-gunned the fleeing refugees using Stuka aircraft fitted with 'screamers', i.e. sirens that made loud screaming noises to further add to the panic.

People today, when they are told about the threat of invasion, often ask, 'Were you frightened?' The honest answer is an emphatic 'No'. Boys of eight upwards are not frightened by such things; at least they weren't during the Second World War. In fact, we found it all very exciting. At every opportunity I would set off to 'inspect' the defences, together with John and our evacuee friend Brian Maystone, who at first was billeted with the stationmaster at Pulborough.

One day we walked along the main road to the hamlet of Hardham, where we knew that a concrete gun emplacement had just been built. They were erected by civilian contractors acting on orders from the military. Once completed they were left unguarded, usually in fields or behind roadside hedges. We boys saw it as our duty to keep an eye on them, not that anyone could steal them – they were far too big and had been solidly built to stand up to enemy gunfire.

Imagine our surprise to find that the new one at Hardham had been built facing the wrong way. They were designed so that a mobile 25lb gun could be run inside them and fire through an aperture in the front wall. When we went in and looked through the slit of that one we realised that it was facing Pulborough. We could clearly see the parish church and its surrounding houses and we knew that was where our defending soldiers would be if the invaders came. So if the Germans had got control of that gun emplacement, they could have wheeled a gun in there and bombarded Pulborough in relative safety.

We were so concerned about that gun emplacement we rushed back to the shop to tell my foster father about it. His response was to laugh, saying, 'Oh you boys and your wild ideas. Don't you think that the Army know what they are doing!' I still believed we were right and a week or so later I heard a loud explosion coming from the direction of Hardham. Later in the shop they told me that the gun emplacement there had been blown up by soldiers from the Canadian Army camp at Petworth. Unfortunately the blast from the explosion smashed most of the windows in the nearby cottages, much to the annoyance of their owners. I wanted to say to my foster father, 'I told you so!' but thought better of it.

The Canadian soldiers who were camped in the grounds of Templemead had the use of two open-topped speed boats in which they carried supplies up the River Arun to another camp near Stopham. The river was, and still is, very shallow at its edges and is not really suitable for fast boats, but the soldiers would race up the river with the boats engines at full throttle, sending a high wave of water splashing right over the banks. That was not popular with many of the local men, because they said it ruined their fishing. I tried several times to get a ride on one of those boats, but the older evacuee girls from Peckham Central School always managed to get there first.

By July 1940 the news about the war became worse by the hour. France had signed a peace treaty with Germany, Italy had joined the Nazis and declared war on Britain, the Channel Islands had been invaded and the swastika flew over public buildings in Guernsey, Jersey, Alderney and Sark. The invasion of Britain was expected at any time. My foster mother was a very shy, nervous woman who never served in the shop, but worked very hard in the back room making hundreds of cups of tea, preparing lunches for the farmers and auctioneers on market days, as well as caring for her family and me. Her only outings were to visit her father and sister on Wednesday afternoons, that being early closing day for the shop. They lived in a tiny cottage at a place called Mare Hill, which is on the outskirts of Pulborough. To get there she would travel on a Southdown bus.

Wooden boathouse at Templemead, 1921. (Vine Collection)

Because she was such a nervous person she became terrified by the threat of invasion. If she heard a distant clap of thunder she would say in an alarmed voice, 'They're on the coast!', thinking that the thunder was the sound of gunfire. To my lasting regret I used to join in with the teasing she got from my foster father and Gwen.

Some unexplained things happened in West Sussex during 1940. At Park Farm, Pulborough, there were two little wooden bungalows that had been lived in for several years by two men. One was said to be an author who lived there when writing his books because of the peace and quiet it gave him. The other man was said to be an artist or an ornithologist, although at the time I had no idea what that was. There was quite a distance between the two bungalows; one had a fantastic view of the South Downs, and the other was in a hollow below where a big gun emplacement was built.

On one of our many walks I noticed that both of the bungalows were closed up and that weeds were taking over their normally well-cared-for little gardens. Rumours about the two men soon began to spread; some people said that they were both German spies and had been arrested. Kinder people said that as they were both of military age they had simply been called up. I never did find out the true story, but I hardly think they could have been spies; their bungalows were in such a remote location I wonder what would they have found to spy on, apart from the building of the gun emplacement of course.

The arrival of tanks in the area created great problems. Some of them were so huge they straddled the narrow Sussex lanes, as they were then. Hard to manoeuvre, they knocked down or damaged many walls and fences, and negotiating the awkward junctions, such as Pulborough's Swan Corner, was very difficult. They were not the things to suddenly encounter in a narrow part of the village or along a country lane. The bren gun carriers were smaller, but their caterpillar tracks also caused a lot of damage. One day a driver lost control as he brought a tank down the steep Church Hill. It rapidly gained speed and he was unable to stop it from crashing through a stone wall at the bottom of the hill and dropping down into a disused workshop below. Fortunately, the workshop was not in use because the man who normally worked there has recently been called up for military service. However, a machine-gun post that had been built behind the wall in readiness for the expected invasion was totally destroyed.

Stopham, a hamlet about a mile west of Pulborough, has a stone bridge that is many centuries old. It is a beautiful structure, but very narrow. Nowadays it is barred to traffic, for which a new bridge has been built nearby, but during the war all traffic had to squeeze over the old bridge, including the tanks. To this day you can still see the grooves that were gouged out of the stone walls by the tanks, even though they are now virtually covered by lichen. Old Stopham Bridge and its surroundings have an atmosphere of great tranquillity; the nearby White Hart inn also has a long history. The bridge was built in 1423 to provide a safe crossing of the River Arun, which at this point is quite deep and when in flood is very wide.

After heavy storms the water flows down through Stopham in torrents and the builders of the bridge had to ensure that it did not obstruct the flow. They therefore provided it with no less than seven arches. However, in 1792 a group of entrepreneurs constructed a navigable canal to link the River Arun with the River Wey, thereby creating an inland route from Littlehampton on the south coast to London and its docklands. The canal was never really successful and suffered badly from the many floods. By 1871 it was derelict, but the high centre arch of Stopham Bridge still reminds anyone who knows its history that it was altered to allow cargo-carrying boats to pass through even when the river was in flood.

Of course as a young evacuee I didn't know any of the above dates, but my foster father had told me about the old canal. Apparently when he was a very young man he had worked as a labourer helping to build the London to Arundel railway, the route of which cut through a tunnel on the old canal. He also remembered cargo-carrying boats coming up the River Arun from Littlehampton to moor at wharves in Pulborough, some of which are still remembered by the names of new developments. A cutting off the river led close to the rear of the Swan Hotel, which boats bringing lime from the quarries at Amberley, by the South Downs, used to use. An old barn in the garden of the house where John was billeted still had a chalk floor from those days. Another canal used to run from the Arun, near Stopham Bridge, to Petworth, but apart from an old iron footbridge hiding in deep undergrowth, nothing is left to show that boats used to pass that way. I used to listen avidly to tales about the river and the old canals. Perhaps that is why, many years later, I would own a narrow boat and explore most of the remaining canals in England and Wales.

However, to return to the description of Stopham as I knew it in the 1940s, near to the bridge, but set discretely back from the road, can be seen Stopham House, the historic home of the Barttelot family who came over with William the Conqueror. The grounds of the house still sweep down to the river, where there is a flight of wide, stone steps down to the water and the remains of a boathouse. I remember the late Lady Barttelot opening a summer fete at Pulborough in the grounds of the former Spring Green Lady Guest House. It was a windy day and she had quite a struggle to keep hold of the wide-brimmed hat she was wearing. The fete was one of many held to raise funds for the war effort, so it was very apt that a solitary Hurricane flew over as she spoke.

As I mentioned before, the river at Stopham is quite wide, although much of its area is usually overgrown with bulrushes and other water weeds. Every year a pair of swans used to build a nest there and successfully raise some cygnets and they, or their successors, probably still do. However, one year a summer storm caused the water to rise. Their nest, in which were two cygnets, floated free of the bulrushes and was carried downstream, followed by a pair of swans, each making a plaintive crying noise. There was nothing anyone could do to help them as they would have been attacked by the swans if they had tried. I never heard what became of that family of swans – perhaps they managed to find a safe part of the river.

Sadly the apparent tranquillity of the river at Stopham was the scene of a far more serious tragedy during the Second World War. Due to the ever-busy state of the small living room of my billet I was not generally allowed to stay indoors during the day, not because I was not wanted there but there simply wasn't enough room. Throughout the day people would be calling into the shop for cups of tea and Gwen or my foster father would call out, 'One tea with!' or 'One tea without!', the 'with' or 'without' referring to sugar. For most of the war sugar was tightly rationed, so it could never be left to the customers to help themselves from a sugar bowl. In those days, of course, the little packets of sugar we have nowadays were not available.

The small living room was inevitably taken up with stacks of crockery, teapots, kettles and a hot-water urn. The only form of heating hot water and cooking was by a coal-fired range. In the summer the heat in the small room was almost unbearable. It was no place for a boy to be with his toys or books, so every morning I would be told, 'Go for a walk and don't come back until lunchtime!' After that meal it would be, 'Out you go until teatime!'.

In the summer, when the weather was fine, always being outdoors presented no problem, unless it was raining. During the winter months it was harder; sometimes we, that is John, Brian and I would go and sit by the fire in the station waiting room, but that soon became boring. Most days we would go for long walks, each one invariably developing into some form of adventure. One of my favourite walks took us along the cinder path beside the railway, then along Steppey Lane, quickly passing a partly ruined barn which we had been told was haunted by the ghost of a man who had hanged himself in there. Sometimes there might be cattle or a horse in the barn that made a noise, causing us to run past as fast as we could.

Soon we came to a sunken track that was overhung with trees. It was always eerily quiet along there; the local people told us it was a Roman road that legionnaires used to march along on their way to a fortified camp nearby. So for a short while we became Roman soldiers. At the end of the sunken lane stood one of the big concrete gun emplacements, from which you could see for miles around and especially the road leading to the coast. We would go into it and would pretend that we were British soldiers watching to see if the Germans were coming. It is still there. After that a public footpath led us to Stopham. On one side we had fantastic views over the valley of the River Arun to the South Downs. On the other side were dense woods in which we had a den, but that story comes later.

As we neared Stopham the path led down a steep hill and brought us to the main Pulborough to Fittleworth and Petworth road. On one side was the White Hart inn and next to that was Stopham Bridge, which has pedestrian alcoves in which you could stand in safety from any passing traffic. During the war that was often heavy tanks or bren gun carriers. If anyone had the misfortune to be trapped under their caterpillar tracks they could easily have been killed, or at least lose a leg. We used to dawdle around Stopham Bridge for quite a while watching the slowly flowing river or, if there was a flood, looking for tree branches and other things floating by. If it was a hot day we wished we had some money to buy lemonade from the White Hart.

One day, however, when we arrived at the bridge there were lots of soldiers and policemen stopping any traffic. When they saw us they immediately started shouting at us to go away. We could see soldiers wading and diving into the river and everyone looked very serious, but no one would speak to us other then telling us to go away. When I got back to the shop I told my foster parents about it, but all they could say was that the soldiers were on some sort of training exercise and wouldn't have wanted us boys getting in the way.

Much later, from my hiding place behind the sweet jars, I heard the men in the shop talking in hushed tones about what had happened at Stopham Bridge. Apparently Army experts were testing a newly designed tank that could be driven underwater on the bed of a river or canal and emerge safely up the opposite bank. Therefore, if an advancing force came to a bridge over water that had been blown up, the tank could simply be driven under the water, emerge on the other side and continue on its way. Sadly at Stopham Bridge the tank failed to re-emerge; it had got stuck underwater and the crew inside ran out of air before they could be rescued and some of them died. The local men's theory was that when the central arch of the bridge was altered to allow barges to get through even when the river was in flood, they also dredged a deep channel in the bed of the river. They believed that the tank had dropped into that deep channel and because its tracks were unable to get a grip on the soft mud, it could not move. We never heard the full story of that tragedy because, like so many things that happened in the war, it was all kept secret.

Our walks to Stopham were just one of the many we used to take. Another took us past the Swan Hotel and on to what was locally

Flooding, 1937. (Vine Collection)

called the Causeway, part of the main road, the A29, to Bognor
Regis. The section from Pulborough to Hardham passed over a very
low-lying stretch of agricultural land known as the Brooks which
was, and still is, very prone to flooding. For generations the flood
waters covered the main road, making it impassable for traffic. To
solve that problem the level of the road was raised by several feet
and culverts were built to allow the water to pass under it instead
of over.

Flooding frequently occurred and often without warning, leaving
the farmers without the opportunity to get their cattle and sheep off
the Brooks to higher ground. There are slightly higher parts of the
Brooks that are not at first covered by flood water, onto which the
cattle would all gather. Somehow the farmers had to drive the cattle
off the islands and make them wade through the flood water, either

to higher land or to the waiting cattle trucks parked on the road. That was never easy because the cattle were very reluctant to leave what they thought was their place of safety. The farm dogs could do little to help because the flood water was usually too deep for them.

From the Causeway we used to watch the farm workers struggling to rescue the animals and hear their shouts of 'Hey! Hey! Gerrup, Gerrup!' and other words that cannot be repeated here. The sheep were especially vulnerable and many drowned as their fleeces became saturated with flood water. We often saw dead ones floating alongside the Causeway or tangled on the barbed-wire fences.

During spells of wet weather the Brooks would often flood even before the River Arun had overtopped its banks, but soon that would happen and the whole area became like an inland sea. Most, but not all, of the houses in Pulborough were built on ground above that of the average flood levels, but parts of the old Swan Hotel and other nearby properties were especially vulnerable, as was that part of the main road. When the floods were up we boys spent many hours at Swan Corner watching the fun as some vehicles failed to get safely through.

My foster father told me several tales about past floods. One of them was about when the new Swan Bridge was being built. Apparently the contractors sited their wooden huts and stacks of timber right alongside the riverbank, and when the local people warned them about the flooding they scoffed at the idea, 'Call this a river, it's little more than a stream, we have built bridges over real rivers!' It was a well-known characteristic of true Sussex people that if anyone laughed at them and refused to take their advice, they would simply shrug their shoulders and walk away, but then stand back to watch the fun as their warnings became true.

Work on the new bridge was started and all the wooden scaffolding (there was no steel scaffolding in those days) and the workmen's walkways were erected, but one night the river level rose dramatically and all the stacks of timber, wheelbarrows, tools and huts, together with the erected scaffolding, were swept away

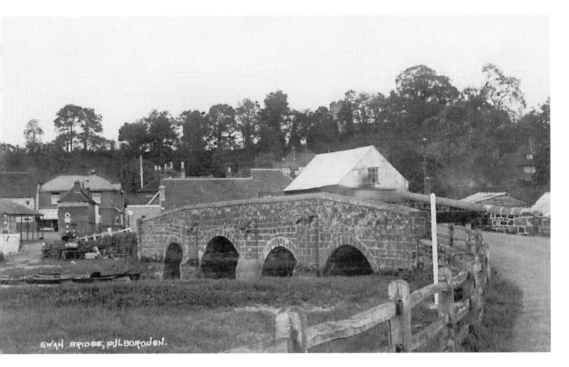

Swan Bridge, 1930. (Vine Colection)

by the fast-flowing water. It is said that many new sheds were built downstream as far away as Amberley during the following few months, using the recovered timber of course.

Another tale about the flooding relates to the Swan Hotel, the oldest parts of which stood on very low ground. The stables would flood first, then water would spurt up from the drains in the yard. That was the signal for flood boards to be placed in the grooves of the kitchen back-door frame and clay packed around them to stop the water from entering. The story is that when a new landlord took over the Swan Hotel, he disregarded the advice from the locals regarding the flooding. During the night the floods came up, no flood boards were fitted, the kitchen was flooded and water gushed down into the beer cellar. The bars were above water level, but that evening floating beer barrels could be heard banging and bumping on the floorboards, much to everyone's amusement, except for the landlord of course.

The Second World War brought more stories about the floods and of people who had ignored the locals' warnings. One story involved the Army. During a period of fine, sunny weather a big military exercise was taking place over much of West Sussex, with most of the activities being centred on places along the stop line, which obviously included Pulborough, with the Swan Hotel being used as command headquarters. Every room in the hotel was commandeered to be used by the officers, with the lower ranks having to eat and sleep under canvas. Their tents were set up in a field situated between the Swan Hotel and the River Arun, with the tanks, bren-gun carriers, jeeps and lorries parked in rows near to the road. In the centre of the camp a large marquee was erected to serve as the cookhouse and mess hall.

Although the weather was still hot and sunny on the day the troops arrived, the signs of a change were clearly visible to those who knew what to look for and I had been taught by my foster father what they were. One thing to look for was how clearly you could see the South Downs. If every detail of them could be seen in sharp focus, for example sheep grazing, there was likely to be a thunderstorm within the next few hours. If you could hear the clacketty-clack of approaching trains even before you could see them, that was another portent of heavy rain. In fact, the signs had been there for several days before the Army arrived – that meant heavy thunderstorms were imminent. The soldiers were told that the River Arun was likely to flood, but they just laughed disbelievingly.

The rain began during the afternoon and continued through the evening and the night. In the early hours of the next morning soldiers sleeping in their tents were awakened by water seeping into them quite rapidly. Soon their sleeping bags and other items were floating and they had to get out of the field as quickly as possible. By dawn the floods were several feet deep and the water had ruined much of the equipment and swamped the engines of the vehicles.

Several weeks passed before everything could be recovered. Of course, there was the knowledge that if the Germans had invaded when the floods were up they could never have reached Pulborough along the main road, because the Causeway and Swan Bridge would have been blown up before they could have used them.

The floods did have some benefits of course, one being that they brought downstream many tree branches and other timber that could be sawn up and used on people's stoves and cooking ranges. It was hard work, first to recover the timber, then to stack it on end to dry, before cutting it with hand saws into manageable sized logs. But when coal was in short supply, as it often was during the war, the logs were a godsend. We evacuee boys spent a lot of our time busy with that work.

Apart from the gun emplacements, machine-gun posts, tank traps and cone-shaped blocks of concrete that were placed ready to use as road blocks, plus all the soldiers, there were no signs in Sussex of actual warfare, but all that was soon to change – the Battle of Britain was about to begin.

7

NEVER IN THE FIELD OF HUMAN CONFLICT

During the summer of 1940 the war situation became ever more serious. Rumours of German landings on the south coast of England were rife and the presence of thousands of soldiers in and around the villages of West Sussex were a source of security, but also created an increasing awareness of the dangers we were in. The Home Guard, initially the butt of considerable ridicule, was now seen in a different light. They were no longer parading in civilian clothes and carrying broom handles instead of rifles, but were an armed and uniformed force, trained and ready to play their part in repelling an invading army.

Rumours abounded regarding the existence of a special, highly secret branch of the Home Guard that was made up of men who would literally 'go underground' if an invading force succeeded in occupying parts of Britain. From my 'listening post' behind the sweet jars I heard low voices talking of men digging hiding places in woods and other secluded places, in which stocks of ammunition, high explosives and food were placed. In the event of an invasion those Home Guard 'specials' would go into their secret hiding places where they would wait until the enemy forces had passed over the area and then emerge under cover of darkness to carry out acts of sabotage, such as blowing up bridges and railway lines, and also killing enemy soldiers. They would do so in the full knowledge that if they were captured they would be tortured and killed. If there were such secret places in or around the Pulborough area, even us inquisitive boys, with our highly developed imaginations, never found them.

However, the Germans knew that an invasion of Britain could only succeed if they had mastery of the air. Somehow they had to destroy the Royal Air Force, or at least render it incapable of mounting serous attacks. Not many miles from Pulborough was the famous RAF fighter base of Tangmere, and situated on the Isle of Wight was the radar station that would detect approaching enemy aircraft and pass the information to the RAF.

Once the Germans had invaded most of France and gained control of the French airfields their aircraft could take off and be over southern England within minutes – too soon for air-raid sirens to sound warnings to the local people. I clearly remember a fine day in 1940 when I set off to walk to school. Already Messerschmitts were weaving and diving over the village and I could hear the rattle of their machine guns and bullets were bouncing along the road and off the roofs of buildings. It appeared that the railway station was their initial target.

If Pulborough ever had an air-raid siren I never heard it and there were certainly no public shelters to run to at that stage of the war. I carried on walking to school, meeting up with John on the way. The enemy planes were still overhead and now appeared to be randomly machine-gunning the village; bullets were thudding into the grass verges beside us. We got as far along Lower Street as the Oasis Cafe, where the owners shouted to us to come in and take cover. They gave us each a glass of lemonade and we stood with them at their back door watching as even more enemy planes flew over.

It was a glorious late summer's day, the sun was shining and there was not a cloud in the sky. The Messerschmitts seemed to be free to fly around as they wished, with no anti-aircraft guns to fire at them. But then we noticed some moving dots very high in the clear blue sky. The dots rapidly grew larger – soon we could see that they were aeroplanes. It then became obvious that they were Spitfires and Hurricanes diving steeply to attack the enemy planes. Within minutes the battle began and we could see a melee of planes weaving and diving to escape or attack. We could hear their engines screaming and their guns firing. Suddenly dense smoke would begin to pour from one of them, then from another. It was obvious that those planes were seriously damaged. If a plane with smoke pouring from it headed due south we knew it was one of the enemies and its pilot was making a desperate attempt to make it back to France, but first it had to gain enough altitude to clear the South Downs. Some failed and we saw them crash into the hillside, when we would cheer and jump for joy, saying, 'That one will never come back to attack us!' We gave no thought to the fact that young men were dying in those crashing planes.

The battle seemed to move away from Pulborough so we left the Oasis Cafe and continued on our way to school, but then the planes came back and we were called into the Post Office to take shelter in their cellar. After a while a postman came down to say that it was now all quiet and we could leave to go to school. When we arrived there, the children were all still sitting on the floor beneath their desks. The school had no air-raid shelters at that time. A teacher was very cross with us, firstly, he said, because we shouldn't have been out while the dogfight was raging and, secondly, because we were late. I never did work out which offence was considered to be the most serious.

During another of the many dogfights that took place over our part of West Sussex during the Battle of Britain, we clearly saw a plane with German markings on its wings drop like a stone and heard it crash into the ground. It had fallen at a remote spot called Toat Hill. The Army raced to the scene, but all they found was wreckage scattered over a wide area, plus the remains of the two-man crew. The story is that a man from Pulborough who kept a butcher's shop volunteered to collect up the remains of the two airmen. Later they were buried with due ceremony by the

Royal Air Force in the churchyard of Pulbourough Parish Church, where they remained for several years before being exhumed and taken to the German War Graves Cemetery near Cannock in Staffordshire. Every week whilst they remained in Pulborough, a local woman would place a small bunch of flowers from her garden on the graves. When asked why she did that, she replied, 'My son was in the RAF and died when shot down over Germany. It is my hope that someone there is doing the same for him.'

One day during the Battle of Britain, we could hear the roar of gunfire coming from the south coast and many believed that the invasion had begun. But the Canadian soldiers camped in the village seemed to be taking no action, and neither was the Home Guard. If the invasion had started why weren't they manning the machine-gun posts and the big gun emplacements, we wondered, and why weren't the road blocks being set up?

We later found out that the sound of gunfire we had heard was not due to an invasion at all, but was coming from the anti-aircraft guns of RAF Tangmere, which was being subjected to an intense attack by German fighters and bombers. Hermann Goering, who at that time was second in command to Adolf Hitler and Supreme Commander of the Luftwaffe, had issued orders that an all-out air attack should be launched upon the fighter bases of the Royal Air Force, of which Tangmere was a prime target. His belief was that if the Spitfire and Hurricane bases were destroyed the Germans would gain the command of the air over Britain, making it possible for the invasion to begin.

Tangmere took a very heavy battering: many of its aircraft were destroyed on the ground, its runways were pitted with bomb craters and many personnel lost their lives. It was initially out of action, but within days its fighter planes were again in the sky, shooting down enemy aircraft. Goering's boastful statements that he would destroy the Royal Air Force were proved wrong and soon after that the planned invasion was postponed and, in fact, never attempted.

The Royal Air Force won the Battle of Britain and Churchill made his famous speech, declaring that:

The gratitude of every home in our island, in our Empire and indeed throughout the world, except in the abodes of the guilty, goes out to the British airmen who, undaunted by odds, unwearied in their constant challenge and mortal danger, are turning the tide of the world war by their prowess and by their devotion. Never in the field of human conflict was so much owed by so many to so few.

I heard that speech on the wireless in the shop. As Churchill spoke everyone crowded in there listened intently, no one made a sound, but when he finished there was spontaneous clapping and cheering.

Many years later, far from West Sussex, I was attending a board meeting of an organisation of which I was the General Secretary. During a coffee break I was talking to the Chairman, who was several years older than me, and as so often happens the talk turned to memories of the war. I told him of hearing the anti-aircraft guns firing to defend Tangmere. To my great surprise the Chairman quietly said, 'I was helping to fire those guns!' That was all he said before calling the meeting to order, but a unique bond had been created between him and me.

Although things became quieter, enemy aircraft still appeared over Sussex and many more were shot down by the Royal Air Force. Often their crews would bail out before their planes caught fire or plunged to the ground. The sight of parachutes floating high above the Sussex countryside naturally attracted great attention. I remember an occasion when one drifted over Pulborough. Several people wanted to know why the Home Guard wasn't trying to shoot it down, but it was pointed out to them that until it reached the ground it was impossible to know whether the man in the rigging was a German or British airman. Besides, we didn't shoot at solitary parachutes, only large clusters of them because they could be Nazi paratroopers.

Another day we saw a parachute drifting over that clearly had no one hanging from it. It did, however, appear to have a fairly large bundle attached to its harness. Again the hotheads wanted it shot down, but a wiser man urged caution, saying, 'If our bullets were to miss the bundle but damage the parachute, that bundle would fall on the village, and if it contains explosives many of us could be killed.' The parachute was left to slowly drift away and I never heard any more about it.

We boys were about to experience much greater excitement. It was a fine day and the three of us set off on one of our longer walks. We had decided to go to Park Farm Woods, where we had a secret den. The woods were dense and very lonely. Some people said they were creepy, but that didn't bother us. Our main concern was to look out for snakes, especially adders, because we knew that their bites were poisonous and could prove quite serious if not treated immediately.

In a very secluded part of the woods, some distance from any footpath, we had built a den using fallen branches covered with a layer of bracken. It was early autumn, so it was easy for us to keep a small stock of apples in the den that we had 'acquired' from someone's garden on the way from the village.

On the day in question we arrived at our den to find that our apples had all gone. Our first reaction was to blame the village boys, but then we wondered why they hadn't destroyed our den while they were there. While we were still arguing about the loss of our apples, John suddenly said, 'There is a man hiding behind a tree over there!' We looked to see where he was pointing, but at first I couldn't see any man and told John he was imagining things. 'I'm telling you there is a man there!' he shouted. Brian saw him before me and said, 'I wonder if he is a German. Has he got a gun?' Then I saw him quite clearly. He looked quite young but was obviously in a very bad way. His clothes were torn and dirty, although we could see they were of a grey colour. As he moved he limped badly and we could see that one leg of his trousers was bloodstained.

'I'm sure he is a German!' John insisted, and we agreed with him. Brian said, 'We had better run back to the village and tell someone.' We hurriedly set off back to the village and went straight into the shop, my billet, where I blurted out, 'There is a German hiding in Park Farm Woods!' There were several customers in the shop at the time and they all started laughing. 'Oh you boys and your fancy ideas,' said my foster father. But we persisted and eventually someone said, 'The boys may be right. I'm passing the police station on my way home so I'll call in and tell them.'

Within an hour a policeman, together with three members of the Home Guard, drove up to Park Farm and went searching for the man. At first they couldn't find any trace of him and began to wonder whether we had indeed let our imaginations run away with us.

The next day the policeman called into the shop to say that they had found the man and he was a German airman. Apparently he was only aged nineteen and his plane had been badly damaged by a Spitfire. His co-pilot was killed and although the plane was still flying, its controls were completely out of action. He decided to bale out and as he hung suspended in the air he saw his aircraft plummet to the ground and crash into a field, where bits of it were scattered over a wide area.

There was a stiff breeze blowing which took him and his parachute many miles away from the crash site. Although very dazed and in shock from the horror of the Spitfire's attack, he was not injured and remained fully conscious as his parachute drifted high above the Sussex countryside. The South Downs drew ever nearer and he could even see the hazy outline of the sea, causing him to fear that he may even be drowned, but suddenly the wind dropped and he found himself plunging down towards a big clump of trees. He made a very bad landing into the trees of Park Farm woods, during which he suffered severe damage to his left leg.

Somehow he had managed to extricate himself and his parachute from the tree. Blood was pouring from his damaged leg and he was in great pain, but he remembered to hide his parachute under some bushes where it could not be seen, just as he and his airmen colleagues had been ordered to do during his training.

By then he was becoming very weak and had great difficulty in walking. He stumbled into our den and hid there. Soon it was dark and very cold. Early the next morning he managed to walk the short distance to the edge of the woods, from where he could see the roofs and chimney pots of Pulborough's houses. Although he badly needed help, he was too scared to try and reach the village because he had been told that any German airman who baled out over England would be instantly shot by the local people. By now he was very hungry, because all he had to eat were the apples that he found in our den.

Suddenly he saw a vehicle coming slowly up the track which led to the woods. It stopped and four men got out. One of them was dressed in a blue uniform; the other three looked like soldiers and carried rifles. They, of course, were the policeman and three members of the Home Guard who had been sent to look for him on the basis of what we had said in the shop.

He tried to run deeper into the woods, but they saw him and shouted to him to stand still, not that he could understand English. The Home Guardsmen pointed their rifles at him, but didn't shoot. He raised his arms in surrender, but collapsed to the ground before they reached him. They gently carried him to their vehicle and drove slowly to the main road, then at high speed to the police station where they laid him on a bunk in one of the cells.

When he began to regain consciousness they gave him a cup of strong tea that the policeman's wife had made for him. They tried to make him understand that they had sent for an ambulance to take him to hospital, but he was still afraid that they were really going to shoot him. Eventually the ambulance arrived and he was taken away. The next morning the policeman called into the shop and told me the above details, adding that we had probably saved that young man's life.

We never heard any more about him and I often wonder whether he survived the war. I hope he did, because he was no more responsible for that terrible war than we boys were. Years later I tried to find out about him, but without success. At first I contacted the German embassy in London, but was told they had no relevant records. Then I tried to locate the wartime records of Pulborough Police Station, but again drew a blank. I was told that such records had been lost. Perhaps someone better at such research may have better luck than me.

8

NOW CAME THE BOMBERS

In September 1940 the sounds of the Royal Air Force and the Luftwaffe fighting over West Sussex were being added to by the nightly throbbing of German bombers flying at high altitudes as they made their way to drop explosives and fire-creating incendiary bombs on London. This created fresh dangers for the southern county areas which lay under the bombers' flight paths. Not all of the Heinkels reached their London target area – some turned back, their pilots 'persuaded' by the British anti-aircraft fire not to risk flying in any further. They then jettisoned their bombs before crossing back over the Channel to their bases.

Hardham Mill, near Pulborough, received a direct hit, but many bombs fell harmlessly in the fields, creating craters that would soon fill with water, often to the intense annoyance of the farmers. 'If I 'ad wanted a pond in my field I'd 'ave dug it meself! Who is going to fill it in? That's what I want to know!' shouted one irate farmer in the shop one market day.

However, the London Blitz brought great worries to all the evacuees. 'Are my parents still alright?' they wondered. 'Is my home still there?' It became a regular occurrence at school to see a policeman appear at the classroom door. The teacher would go to him and they would speak to each other very quietly. Then the teacher would go to one of the evacuees and take him or her out of the classroom. We didn't need to hear or to be told what had been said. We knew that yet another child had probably had the news broken to them that their parents had been killed in the bombing and their home totally destroyed.

I never worried that such a thing could happen to my parents. In my mind they were invincible. They did in fact survive the Blitz, but their house, in common with most others, suffered considerably from the blast of bombs that fell nearby. Its windows were blown in, its heavy Victorian plaster ceilings came crashing down and doors no longer fitted. Gaps in the long rows of terraced houses appeared in most roads after the heavy raids.

I also never thought about what might have happened to me if I had lost my parents. I knew that some of the affected evacuees went away to live with grandparents or aunts and uncles after receiving the tragic news. One evening, during the height of the London Blitz, my foster father quietly told me, 'If the worst should happen in London, we will adopt you.' At the time I didn't understand what it was he was trying to tell me, but in recent years I have realised the full meaning of his words. He was not a man who could easily communicate with children, or to show any signs of affection, but he had clearly thought about what could happen to my family and was trying to reassure me that I would be looked after like one of his own family.

Not everyone in the village was quite as understanding about the evacuees' worries. I heard that some foster parents were taking their evacuees with them to high ground at night and pointing to the red glow in the sky of London burning. They clearly did that without thinking of the effect it must have had on the children whose homes and families were in London, perhaps in an area that was on fire.

On 4 October 1940 a death from enemy bombing occurred in the Pulborough area, when in broad daylight the rector of the nearby hamlets of Stopham and Hardham was killed by a German bomb as he was travelling between his two parishes. I always believed that he was driving his car along the Stopham to Pulborough road, but others say he was riding a bicycle. The section of road where the tragedy occurred has since been bypassed due to road realigning and widening, but it is possible to see the memorial tablet set in a stone wall which bears the words, 'Near this spot William Beech Masefied (late Chaplain RN) for seven years rector of the parishes of Stopham and Hardham, was killed by enemy action on the 4th October 1940.' The Revd W.B.Masefield was the brother of the then Poet Laureate. His name is engraved on the Stopham War Memorial that stands opposite the church.

Two years after the death of Revd Masefield, a greater tragedy was to occur. On 29 September 1942, in a daylight raid, a German bomber scored a direct hit on the building of the boys' school in the ancient market town of Petworth. The school was reduced to a heap of rubble and twenty-six young boys, their headmaster and another teacher all lost their lives. The noise of the explosion was heard all over the little town and the surrounding countryside. In fact I heard it at Pulborough, five miles away.

One of the first people to arrive on the scene of the devastation was the then Vicar of Petworth, who immediately began to search for survivors. Very quickly the tragic news reached a nearby Canadian Army camp and the soldiers rushed to the site and began digging in the rubble with their bare hands in hope of finding some of the boys still alive.

A few days later Canadian soldiers lined the narrow streets of the town as a long convoy of Canadian Army trucks slowly drove to the cemetery, carrying the small coffins of the boys. They were all buried in a long grave, at the head of which stands a tall, white stone cross bearing the words:

In loving memory of the
Headmaster, teacher and boys
who lost their lives when
Petworth Boys School
was bombed on the
29th September 1942

The names of the boys are engraved on small tablets set along the curbing of the mass grave.

The small town of Petworth has never fully recovered from such a disaster and a memorial service is held every year in the parish church. Sadly the cemetery in which the boys were buried is now disused, the former chapel is derelict and the tree-lined pathways are overgrown. Someone does cut the grass around the boys' communal grave, but to get to it is difficult. In the author's opinion this grave should be placed under the care and maintenance of the War Graves Commission, so giving those children who were the innocent victims of war the official recognition they so rightly deserve.

9

THE HIGHS AND LOWS OF A SCHOOLBOY'S WAR IN SUSSEX

Many years have passed since I, as an eight-year-old boy, was uprooted from the security, love and certainties of my family home and taken to live with strangers in a totally different environment. Not all children living in the 1930s were as fortunate as me; just as there are today, there were many families living in poor homes. Unemployment was rife and at school it was commonplace to see children with pinched faces, wearing ill-fitting, cast-down clothing, smelling of poverty.

Along the busy shopping streets, such as Peckham's Rye Lane, unemployed ex-servicemen who had become disabled during the First World War could be seen shuffling along carrying trays of matchboxes that they hoped to sell for a few pence. Others would be singing the wartime songs, with their cap held out for people to drop in a coin.

None of those disadvantages applied to me. My father had a regular job and my mother did not have to go out to work to supplement the family's income so she was always there to care for us. We lived in a five-bedroomed house situated in a quiet, tree-lined road. It was not modern by today's standards, for example it lacked central heating and relied upon gas for lighting and cooking, but we had space and security.

I suppose many people would say we were lucky compared to lots of other families at that time, but I have never been able to accept the premise that success is entirely dependent upon luck. It was not luck that gave my father regular employment and therefore the financial means to provide for his family. He had been a soldier in the First World War and was gassed and injured. When peace came he found himself among the many thousands of unemployed men looking for work. His solution was to arrive early at the gates of the London docks to join the hundreds of other men hoping to be picked for a day's work. Not everyone was lucky enough to be picked, and those who were not simply had to walk away with no money. It was known as the casual labour scheme.

Perhaps there was an element of luck whether a man was picked or not. However, the people who stood at the dock gates pointing to the men selected to work for them that day knew who were the good workers and those who were not. Naturally the good workers were picked first. My father must have become noted as a good worker and was soon offered a permanent job by one of the warehouse companies, thus ensuring his a regular weekly wage.

In addition to working full time (which in those days was five-and-a-half days every week), he also took on an allotment on which he grew vegetables to help feed his family. That was long before the war and its 'Dig for Victory' campaign. He was also an accomplished shoe repairer and spent many hours soling and heeling our shoes.

Our mother originated from Robertsbridge in East Sussex and was one of a large family that lived in a small, end-of-terrace cottage, which in her childhood days was very primitive. Her father was the local carrier, delivering parcels throughout the area that had arrived by train at Robertsbridge Station. He owned a team of horses and was a very well-known local character. Sadly, when motor-driven vans became popular, he refused to modernise and his business failed. He then became a porter working for the Kent & East Sussex Light Railway at its Robertsbridge terminus.

Due to her rural upbringing, it was second nature to our mother to cook good meals using vegetables from the allotment and to know how to buy the best items from the stallholders that lined the side streets of Rye Lane, Peckham.

They made a good team, my mother and father, and brought up their five children to know and understand the ethics of hard work, reliability and responsibility, which were to help us cope with the hardships and traumas we would encounter during the Second World War. Above all they gave us a sense of security that was to sustain those of us who became evacuees. There was always the knowledge that if things got really bad for us whilst we were evacuated, we could, in an emergency, call upon them and they would come.

Fortunately such a situation never arose for the three of us who were evacuated to Pulborough, but for our brother Ernest, who was evacuated with his school to Shoreham, things did go badly wrong and when our mother visited him she found he was in a poor state of health, desperately unhappy and living with indifferent foster parents. She promptly took him home and nursed him back to good health. He was never re-evacuated, but survived unscathed throughout the London Blitz and the rest of the war.

Coming, as I did, from such a secure family background, certain facets of the evacuation and the war were very hard for me to understand and I experienced many highs and lows during the four years I was away from home. The first low came on the day we were evacuated. To me the walk to the railway station, the hustle and bustle that happened there, the shouting of the porters and teachers as they tried to keep us back from the edge of the platform, followed by the protracted 'stop/start' of the train journey to Pulborough, was all part of a great adventure.

It didn't bother me when they crammed us all into the pens of the cattle market, neither did the cursory medical examination in which a woman yanked a comb through my hair and disinfectant trickled down my neck. But when the people who were to be foster parents came into the school things took an unexpected turn for the worse. They had been told earlier that morning, 'The evacuees are on their way. Come to the school to pick which one or ones you will take into your homes!'

We all had to sit on the floor of the classroom and wait to be chosen and because I thought a man was pointing at me I stood up when he said, 'I'll take that one!', only for him to say, 'No, not you. I want the boy behind you.' Never before, in my young life, had I experienced such a positive rejection.

The story of my first billet and subsequent move to the family with whom I was to live for the next four years has already been told. My reception there was a real high. They seemed pleased to have me. I was immediately given a cup of tea and a slice of fruit cake. Even Dinah the dog, who I discovered usually had no time for strangers, wagged her tail when she saw me. Mickey, the big tabby cat, came in to look at me and we were soon to become close friends.

Starting to attend Pulborough Village School, after a few wonderful weeks of freedom to explore the Sussex countryside, brought what were to me inexplicable incidents of rejection. Probably the first was when it was pointed out to me that although I had been evacuated with my sister's school, I was not really part of it. As its name clearly stated, Peckham Central Girls' School was not intended to have boy pupils. In any case, it was for children aged eleven and over and I was only eight. Therefore I and the other evacuee boys were placed with the village school where the reception from the local boys, and even some of the teachers, was far from welcoming.

It was commonplace for the foster parents to refer to us as 'Our evacuee' and for us to be introduced to people as that, rather than by our name. Due to the many false myths that had spread in the reception areas about the evacuees even before we arrived, it was to be expected that some people looked upon us with a high degree of suspicion, perhaps even apprehension. Many really did believe that we were all delinquent street urchins from inner-city slums. Just what my parents would have thought if they had known that some of their children were being so categorised I hate to think.

One of the worst examples of such an attitude that I experienced happened at, of all places, Pulborough Rectory. In those days the rector of Pulborough lived in the mansion now known as the

Old Rectory. The rector at that time was the Revd Frost, known by the farm workers and many others who came into the shop where I was billeted as 'Owld Frosty the Parson'. To them the rector was an aloof person who employed housemaids, gardeners and a cook. He was taken everywhere in a chauffeur-driven car and if anyone wanted to arrange a baptism, wedding or funeral they had to go to the curate's house, not the Rectory. Owld Frosty certainly never called at the shop for a cup of tea, a bar of chocolate or a packet of cigarettes.

The Rectory stood in extensive grounds which included a tennis court, herbaceous borders, a vegetable garden, an orchard, manicured lawns and a lake. Normally they were kept strictly private, but once a year a garden fete was held there to raise money for various charities. Many people took the opportunity to visit the Rectory gardens, walk along its gravel paths and admire the beautiful surroundings.

In common with all local events, posters about the open day were brought to the shop to be displayed. My foster parents were always reluctant to attend any events, using the ever-open shop as their excuse. But now they had got me to send, which I welcomed. The day of the Rectory garden fete arrived and I was told to polish my shoes and wear my Sunday suit. After being checked to see that my hair was combed and my fingernails clean, I set off to meet Brian, my evacuee friend, who was also going.

We arrived at the Rectory and, after paying for our tickets at the garden gates, we had set off to walk slowly along the paved terrace at the rear of the house when we heard voices behind us. One of the speakers was clearly that of the rector saying, 'Mary, are the French windows locked? We don't want those boys going into the house, do we?' Mary, whoever she was, replied, 'Oh yes, but I am sure they won't do that!' To which Owld Frosty said, 'You must make sure because those boys are only evacuees and won't know any better!'

On hearing that, Brian and I turned round and walked out of the Rectory grounds, probably muttering, 'You can keep your rotten fete!' How Owld Frosty even knew that we were evacuees is inexplicable, because as far as we knew he had never before met us.

He never, as far as we were aware, visited the village school, even though it was a Church of England one, to give talks on religion or to conduct prayers – that was done by his curate.

Years later I learnt that the Revd Frost and his family actually worked very hard for the war effort, serving on numerous committees and organising many fundraising events. I believe he also held hospitality dinners at the Rectory for senior officers of the Canadian Army and the headmistress of the Peckham Girls Central School when they were billeted in the area. But he clearly never really understood we evacuee boys.

Not everyone in my evacuation area was indifferent to us. I am particularly fond of my memory of one very caring lady who I often met as she cycled through the village. When she saw me she always stopped to speak. Sometimes she would place her hands on my shoulders and, with her piercing blue eyes, look hard into mine, saying, 'Hullo my dear, are you alright? If ever there is anything wrong, or you are worried about something, you will tell me, won't you?' She was actually the district nurse, whose job it was to care for the sick and the elderly over a very large area. She lived in a tiny cottage along Lower Street, which has sadly since been demolished to make way for more modern housing. I shall never forget her: she really understood and cared about us evacuees.

As the weeks of being away from home slipped into months and the months became years, so the country way of life and the beautiful Sussex countryside began to have a lasting effect upon me. The seasons became more important and the cycles of gardening, farming and the weather became of ever-greater interest to me. I began to concern myself with whether there was going to be a late frost and, if so, did I need to earth up the shoots of the early potato crop? Would the fine weather hold long enough for the sheaves of corn to dry? Had I shut up the hen houses properly so that the 'owld fox' couldn't break in and kill the roosting poultry?

I also became aware of the different types of fish that could be seen swimming in the clear, fast-flowing waters of the River Arun; of the views of the South Downs that changed according to the weather; and of Chanctonbury Ring high on a crest. I noticed the magical scents of the countryside after rain, or at dusk after a hot summer's day. My way of speaking also changed as I lost my South London accent and gained a Sussex one in its place. I became a country boy.

Of course, I never forgot my parents or that my real home was not in Sussex, but in the crowded district of Camberwell in South London. Homesickness was still ever present, but now I rarely cried myself to sleep in the darkness of my bedroom at night. But all too often and unexpectedly something would trigger it off and I would be overcome with emotion. It could be something quite simple, such as seeing a London-bound train.

One of my daily jobs was to carry heavy cans of drinking water from the shop to the chicken runs, which were some distance away. The route took me along a cinder path that ran beside the railway. I could see the signal gantry in the near distance and if the arm was raised for the 'up' line I knew a train would soon be passing, so I would put the cans down and wait to count the carriages. If there were only five I knew it was a local train that would probably terminate at Horsham, but if there were twelve or thirteen carriages it was heading for London and I would look wistfully at the people sitting inside, wishing that I was with them and going home. The tears would flow, but when the train had gone, it was time to pick up the cans and continue on my way to look after the chickens. Of course I never told anyone about it, but remembered instead my mother's words, 'Big boys don't cry!'

However, on one unforgettable occasion, and to my acute embarrassment, my pent-up emotions became very public. One of the regular customers at the shop was the driver of a Southdown bus on the route between Brighton and Midhurst which would stop for about ten minutes at Pulborough to connect with the trains. He would call in at the shop for a quick cup of tea. It so happened that he lived at Storrington, not very far from Pulborough, and was a member of a local choral society that was putting on an evening of songs and music in the near future at Pulborough Village Hall.

To my great surprise he asked me if I would like to go; my foster father gave his permission and I was presented with a complimentary ticket. I was aged about ten at the time and had never before been to such a show. The evening of the concert eventually came and I felt so grown up as I walked from the shop through the village to the hall, carefully clutching my ticket. When I showed my ticket at the entrance door I was immediately led to a reserved seat in the second row at the front. I felt so very important and I heard someone whisper to the person next to them saying, 'Who is that boy?' and the answer given was, 'He is the evacuee at Burchell's shop.' I pretended not to have heard.

Then the lights were dimmed, the big velvet curtains slowly opened and there, on the stage, was the choir, all dressed in red, white and blue costumes. They sang many songs, most of which I had never heard before. During the interval someone bought me a glass of lemonade from the bar and I was so very happy. It was during the final part of the show that, for me, everything went wrong. All the members of the choir were grouped on the stage singing the popular Second World War songs, such as 'White Cliffs of Dover', 'Run Rabbit' and many more, with all the audience joining in, including me. But as the show neared its end, the lights were dimmed and the music became softer as the choir sang the songs that my parents used to sing together as they sat by the fireside on Saturday evenings. Songs such as 'Red Sails in the Sunset', 'When I Grow too Old to Dream', 'Daisy, Daisy, Give Me Your Answer Do'. Finally they sang 'Keep the Home Fires Burning' and 'Be It Ever So Humble, There's No Place Like Home'. That totally broke my composure and the tears poured down my face. Try as I might, I couldn't stop crying and sobbing. Fortunately the lights were still dimmed, but suddenly there was a loud crash on the drums, all the lights came on and everyone stood to sing the National Anthem. Still I couldn't stop crying and I was aware that people were looking at me.

As soon as the music stopped I tried to get out of the hall as quickly as possible. One woman was obviously concerned and tried to put her arm around my shoulders, saying 'Are you alright?' To my lasting regret I pushed her away in my struggle to get out of the hall into the dark anonymity of the blackout, where nobody could see me crying.

By the time I got back to the shop I had calmed down. Only my foster mother was there and if she could see I had been crying it was not mentioned. I had my usual glass of milk and two digestive biscuits before going to bed, where I cried a lot more. The next morning I was worried that the woman I had so rudely pushed away at the end of the concert might come into the shop to complain about me. But if she did, nothing was ever said to me about it.

That episode was one of the big downs in my life as an evacuee; the next day I went for a long walk in the Sussex countryside, which now meant nearly as much to me as my memories of home. I returned from my walk feeling much better and again able to come to terms with what it was really like to be an evacuee and to cope with that ever-present homesickness.

In common with most of the children who were evacuated in September 1939, I firmly believed that I would be home again by Christmas. In fact, when my parents were telling me about the pending evacuation, my father had clearly said, 'You have nothing to worry about and you will be home by Christmas!'

When in early December the teachers at Pulborough Village School said they wanted me to act in the play they were planning for Christmas, I said I couldn't do that because I would be back in London by then. As 25 December drew nearer I began gathering holly with bright red berries from the hedgerows ready to take home with me. When we made Christmas cards I said I would not have to post mine to my parents because I could take them with me.

Imagine my devastation when I was told that I would not be going home for Christmas after all. The government had announced that evacuees should be left in the reception areas and parents were strongly urged not to bring their children home. The evacuated teachers had their holidays cancelled and were ordered to organise parties and entertainment for the evacuees so as to keep them occupied.

Village hall being used as a cinema in 1944. (WS CRO Garland N 23991)

My foster parents made every effort to compensate for me not being allowed to go home. Even the shop was closed on Christmas Day, but when I realised that many of the other evacuees had gone home I was very upset. After Christmas it became very clear why the government had tried to keep the evacuees in the reception areas. When schools reopened after the holiday they found that many of the evacuees were missing because they had not returned from their homes, which was exactly what the government did not want to happen.

I did not go home for Christmas in 1940 or 1941, so when I heard that I would be allowed to make a very short visit in 1942 I was wildly excited. My foster father always killed several chickens just before Christmas to sell to his regular customers. It was my job to help him catch the ones destined for the oven and then to pluck their feathers, taking great care not to tear their skins in the process. One of the chickens would be sent to my parents.

10

School in a Hall and Other Places

In Chapter 5 I mentioned that although we evacuee boys had to attend the village school, the headmistress of Peckham Central Girls' School had secured the use of Pulborough Village Hall in which to teach her girls. It was some while before that could happen and during that period everyone's education became very disrupted, including that of the local children. A two-shift system was tried, but found to be hopelessly inadequate. There were simply too many pupils for the small school building to cope with.

The teachers used to take us around the country lanes on what they called nature walks, or local history studies. Of course it was good for us to learn about such things, but with no books or exercise papers to refer to it was all rather hopeless. If it rained we spent the time huddled in barns.

Miss Ambler, the determined headmistress of the Peckham Central Girls' School, had to fight hard to persuade the two education authorities, namely those of London County Council and West Sussex County Council, of the desperate need for premises and to make them agree to meet the costs of hiring the village hall. Although the majority of the local people wanted to do their best for the evacuees, the Village Hall Committee had to ensure that it would still be available for use by other organisations.

Eventually a compromise was reached that secured the use of the hall during the day for the girls' school on the understanding that everything was cleared away at the end of each afternoon so that it was available in the evenings and weekends for the usual events, such as dances, concerts, lectures and other such meetings.

Initially all the evacuee boys would attend the village school because they were under the age of eleven and therefore too young to attend a central school. However, many of them reached that age while they were still evacuees and so they were permitted to attend the central school, provided they had passed the necessary examination. Three years had to pass before I was old enough to attend the central school in the village hall. I don't remember ever sitting for an examination, but I suppose I must have done.

Although it provided the only possible solution to the problem of educating more children than was possible in the village school, the hall was never designed or intended to be used as a school. Inevitably most of the building comprised the actual hall, but there was also a stage with small dressing rooms on either side. Under the stage was a fairly large room that was used as a licensed bar when dances were held and for other catering uses. Above the main entrance was the projection room, in which cameras could be set up to show films. It had apertures in its inner wall through which the films could be projected onto a screen set up on the stage at the end of the hall. Once a week a man would come with his equipment to put on a film show. Mobile cinemas were very popular in those days when the nearest proper ones involved a bus ride from Pulborough to either Petworth or Arundel.

There were toilets and cloakrooms on either side of the main entrance to the hall and outside was a field which could be used for games and as a playground. It also had swings, which were very popular. Trestle tables were set up on both sides of the hall, around which the pupils sat. The only equipment for the teachers to use was a blackboard for each table. The two dressing rooms were also used for small groups and the projection room was where the girls learnt to type, the theory being that it would contain the inevitable clattering noise of the typewriters. However, it was soon found necessary to block off the projection apertures to prevent the girls from pulling faces at the pupils in the hall below.

The room under the stage was used as another classroom, usually for current affairs, which in those days was all about the war. There were large maps on which little paper flags could be pinned showing the countries that had been invaded by the German and Italian armies and where the Allied troops were fighting, the flags being moved according to their progress or retreat.

Due to the need to leave the hall clear every afternoon, the trestle tables had to be taken down and stacked away, with the chairs being set out in rows or around the sides. Pupils had to carry all their books and papers to and from their billets in heavy satchels every day. During school hours the only place to hang the satchels was on the backs of the chairs, but when a child stood up the chair would immediately tip over and make a clattering noise, much to the annoyance of the teachers.

When I finally started attending the central school in the village hall, I found it was very difficult not to pay more attention to what the teacher at the next table was saying rather than my own. I was frequently in trouble over that. It was not a really satisfactory way to run a school, but there was no better alternative. However some lessons were held in other premises, one of them being the club room of the Five Bells public house. It was there that I was first introduced to classical music by a young woman who had come straight from a teachers' training college.

She was to teach us music – a mixed class of boys and girls, most of whom only knew the popular songs of the wartime era and the dance music of bands such as those led by Victor Sylvester, Joe Loss, Henry Hall, Billy Cotton and the famous American band leader Glen Miller. The only equipment she had was her own wind-up gramophone and a few 78' records. But to her credit she managed to teach us how to appreciate music such as the *1812 Overture*. This was achieved against a backdrop of advertisements proclaiming that 'Guinness is good for you!' and others telling us how good Bulmers Cider and Friary Ales were, not forgetting that Craven A cigarettes were soothing to the throat.

Another most unlikely building in which lessons were held was that of the former almshouses, located at the lych-gate entrance to Pulborough parish churchyard. Lych-gates are ancient structures that are roofed, but open at the sides, apart from low stone-built walls on which the coffins could be placed whilst the mourners awaited the arrival of the priest. As Pulborough Church stands at the top of a steep hill, the pallbearers were no doubt very grateful for the opportunity to have a rest before carrying the coffin into the church.

For us schoolchildren the lych-gate provided a good place to wait until we could go into the old adjoining building for what they called domestic science lessons. Domestic science was considered to be a very important subject in girls' schools and as we boys were attending one, albeit not of our choice, we also had to attend such lessons whether we liked it or not.

The almshouses were originally intended to provide retirement homes for elderly people, but were given over for the evacuees' school use in the early weeks of the war. Two retired lady teachers were found to teach domestic science. However it was soon realised that many of the evacuees had been billeted in cottages that were too far from the village for them to go to and fro for their lunches; therefore school dinners had somehow to be provided for them. Such a thing had never been considered for the local children, no matter how far away they lived. They had to bring sandwiches and eat them sitting at their desks in the classroom. That was years before the present school-dinner system had been even thought of, least of all operated.

The two elderly ladies who ran the domestic science lessons in the old almshouses made it perfectly clear that they resented having to teach boys – perhaps they never had to in all their years of being teachers. They ruled us with 'a rod of iron' and usually only gave us very menial jobs to do, such as cleaning their shoes and scrubbing the stone-flagged floors. However they must have found me to be fractionally less objectionable than the other boys and decided to teach me how to make custard in a big iron saucepan. I was constantly watched and would be in serious trouble if I failed to stir it vigorously enough to prevent it sticking and burning at the bottom of the pan.

Pupils attending domestic science lessons in the mornings had to prepare and cook the lunches. Those present in the afternoons found it was their lot to wash all the plates, dishes, cutlery and pans that had been used and to scrub the wooden tables (there were no formica surfaces in those days). Considering how lacking in space and modern facilities the old almshouses were, it was remarkable how those two ladies managed to produce such good lunches, in spite of the rationing and shortages, in addition to being forced to tolerate boys in their classes.

Without exception the war, with its shortages of books, paper and other materials, brought problems to all schools. Even worse, they found that many of their teachers were called up for military service. Perhaps the hardest hit were those in the places the government had designated as reception areas for evacuees. Many of them found their number of pupils on roll had doubled or even trebled overnight once the evacuees had arrived.

Differences inevitably arose between the head teachers of schools in the reception areas and those of the evacuated schools, who quite naturally made every effort to maintain control over their pupils and the traditions of their schools. It was extremely difficult for everyone involved and the education of both evacuees and the local children in the reception areas suffered because of the war. In my opinion the teachers should have been awarded some token of official recognition for what they did, but in common with the evacuees they were overlooked at the end of the war.

11

Trains and Things That Went 'Clank' in the Night

Even before I was evacuated trains and railways held a great fascination for me. Through the chinks in the wooden fence at the edge of my London school playground I could look down upon a railway cutting and see the electric trains passing by on the rails that were kept shiny by the constant use they were subjected to. The many wild flowers that grew on the grassy banks of the embankment made the whole area seem rather like the countryside. Even more exciting for me were the ornate coaches of a luxurious Pullman train that often stood in a siding quite near to my school. From my vantage point I could see the little tables, each covered by an immaculate white cloth. Nearest to the window every table had a little electric lamp, each with a red shade. Sometimes the lamps would be left switched on, making the cutlery gleam and sparkle.

It all looked so luxurious and so different to the austere Victorian school, with its gas lighting, cream and green painted walls, bare floorboards and coke-fired stoves in the corner of each classroom, the fumes from which would make the children whose desks were near them drowsy on winter afternoons. I was enthralled by that Pullman train and when I was told that I might be going away, I used to say, 'When I'm 'vacuated I want to go on that train.' I didn't know then that 'my train' was actually the famous *Brighton Belle* and very different from the one I would be crammed onto for my journey to Sussex.

When I found myself billeted only a few yards away from Pulborough Station, with its goods yard, cattle pens and sidings, I was delighted. I soon got to know the porters and other men who worked on the railway, because they all used to call in the shop for their cups of tea and packets of cigarettes. For a short while my sister Jean was billeted with the family of a signalman who worked in the signal box situated alongside the 'up' line and quite near to the station platforms. Soon we were helping to take his lunch to the signal box.

I was fascinated by the different bells that would ring to advise that a train was approaching and the assortment of levers that had to be used. He wasn't really allowed to have boys in the signal box and sometimes he would say, 'Quick, sit down on the floor!' That was to avoid us being seen by an inspector on a passing train. I never did learn how he knew which train might have an inspector on board.

The goods yard was considered to be a dangerous area, which I was not allowed to enter, but from a footpath running alongside I could watch all the activity. In those days most of the goods needed in the area arrived by train in an assortment of trucks, most having open tops and the names of their owning companies painted on their sides. Coal would arrive from the Kent, Nottinghamshire and South Yorkshire collieries and the local coal merchant's men had to bag it up into hundredweight sacks, then load them onto their lorries, ready to deliver to their customers over a wide area. Sometimes the trucks would arrive filled with sweet-smelling cow cake and other foodstuffs for the many farm animals in the district, for collection by carts pulled by tractors.

Not all of the work in the goods yard was that of unloading; sometimes goods were brought there to be taken away. At certain times of the year the yard was busy handling hundreds of tons of sugar beet. It was brought in on farm carts and trailers, but I don't recall seeing many horse-drawn carts there. On their arrival the carts and trailers were positioned alongside open-topped railway trucks and the laborious process of loading began, mostly carried out by men with specially designed long-handled forks with many prongs. There were a few little conveyor belts set up to speed up the loading, but most was done by hand, and what a back-breaking job it must have been.

My favourite place at the station was the goods shed. In those days parcels could be sent by rail to the nearest station of the recipient. For example, someone in London wishing to send a parcel to a customer living near Pulborough would contact a carrier, such as the famous Carter Pattersons or Thomas Tillings. They would collect the parcel and take it to a railway station and from there it would travel by train to Pulborough, where it would be placed in the goods shed ready to be collected by the local carrier and delivered to the customer. It was a good system, but I believe that delays and breakages were frequent.

In charge of the Pulborough goods shed was a jovial character who had a ready laugh and would joke with everyone. When he came into the shop he would call out, 'Cup of tea for a good porter!' Although my friends and I were not allowed to go into the goods yard, our friend the 'good porter' was always pleased to see us; whether we were a help or a hindrance to him is hard to say.

During 1940 and the invasion scare, the government issued an order that all place names, road signs and anything that may help the invading Germans, if they came, were to be either removed or painted over. People, including us boys, were told that if anyone asked us for directions we were forbidden to assist them because they may belong to the enemy. Those instructions gave us many opportunities for devilment.

Swan Corner, the main Pulborough road junction, was the best place to be for that. Due to the war and petrol rationing there was very little civilian traffic on the roads; in fact, most privately owned cars had been immobilised and laid up for the duration. Their place was taken by the many military vehicles, such as Army lorries, jeeps, bren-gun carriers, tanks and staff cars. Of course, all their drivers had maps and did not need to ask for directions. However, the occasional civilian car might come along and a bewildered driver would shout to us for directions, to which we always responded by sending them completely the wrong way. Many gallons of rationed petrol must have been totally wasted due to us. Our ready excuse if we had been found out was always that we thought the driver was a spy.

At the railway station things were more helpful for the arriving passengers. With all the name plates and other signs removed, it was impossible for passengers to be sure at which station the train had stopped, so the porters were ordered to shout out its name. We joined that with great enthusiasm, shouting 'Pulborough, Pulborough' at the tops of our voices. Sometimes the arriving train was only the single-carriage one from Midhurst, perhaps with no passengers travelling on it, but we shouted just the same.

In those days passenger trains also carried parcels, milk churns, bicycles, cut flowers, baskets of fruit and vegetables and many other such items. All these had to be stacked on the platforms at the exact spot where the guard's carriage would stop. When the train arrived there was a scramble to get all the items on board as quickly as possible, so that it could depart strictly on time.

My greatest interest regarding the railway in my part of West Sussex was in the little steam train that pottered from Pulborough along the single-track branch line to Fittleworth, Petworth and Midhurst. Unlike the quieter electric trains on the main line, this one seemed to be incredibly fussy and noisy. Its arrival at Pulborough always involved whistles and snorts of steam from its engine, followed by prolonged hissing while it was stationary alongside Platform No. 3.

For its return journey to Midhurst, it had to cross the main line under the signalman's instructions. With that safely accomplished it then had to be positioned alongside Platform No. 1 with its engine in reach of the pump that sucked up water from the River Arun below, in order to refill its tank. I never saw any coal being loaded so it must have picked that up at one of the other stations on its route.

With all the routine chores completed and after many glances at the big clock on Platform No. 1, the guard would wave his green flag and, to the accompaniment of more whistles and snorts from the engine, off she would go, down the main line to Hardham Junction and on to its own single-line track. After leaving Pulborough it was only two-and-a-half miles to Fittleworth Station, but that involved crossing the flood plain of the River Arun and its tributary the River Rother, which after heavy rain could turn the fields into a vast lake. Sometimes the water covered the railway line, but the little engine still trundled along pulling its single carriage. It was that which gave it the name of the Midhurst Boat Train, at least by my foster father.

The station after Fittleworth was Petworth, which was located discretely some distance from the ancient town and the stately mansion of Petworth House. Then came Midhurst, a total journey from Pulborough of eleven miles, which our dear little train did eight times a day, each way, every weekday and five times on Sundays.

One day during the Battle of Britain period when there was so much aircraft activity over West Sussex, I was walking along the footpath that runs between Park Farm and Stopham Bridge. The view from that footpath spreads right across the Arun Valley to the South Downs and I could see the Midhurst Boat Train puffing along on its way to Pulborough. As I stood watching it I saw a Messerchmitt come diving down and heard the staccato sound of its guns. It was clearly firing at the Midhurst Boat Train, but it continued to trundle along.

Later that afternoon when I was back at the shop I told everyone what I had seen, but no one knew anything about it. As so often happened, some of the men in the shop just laughed and said I was making it all up. Later that evening I met my friend, the good porter, and told him what I had seen. Instead of laughing disbelievingly he said, 'The branch line train has just come in. Come with me and we'll look to see if there are any bullet holes.' We carefully looked all over the engine and its single carriage, but could find no signs of damage.

'I definitely saw the German plane zoom over and heard its guns firing,' I insisted, expecting the porter to doubt me, but instead his comment was, 'Thank goodness they missed!' Then he checked with the train crew to see if they knew anything about it. Apparently, as was often the case, there were no passengers on the train for that trip. None of the train crew had seen or heard an enemy aircraft but said that was possible because of the noise of the engine and the clatter of its wheels and those of the carriage on the track. We never heard anything more about that wartime incident, of which it seems I was the only observer. Sadly I never travelled on the Midhurst Boat Train and never will. The line was closed in 1966 and its track has been reclaimed by the lush growth of the Sussex countryside.

As for the goods yard at Pulborough Station, it is no longer busy with trucks being loaded or unloaded and now never echoes to the sounds of steam engines, and instead is a car park. It is all so different from how it was during the Second World War, when night after night dozens of Canadian soldiers transferred war weapons and live ammunition from trucks to Army lorries, working in the dim light of shaded oil lamps. Exactly what they were unloading and taking away was a closely guarded secret at the time and never talked about.

12

CUP OF TEA FOR MR WHITEHEAD

It was not generally known, in fact it was a closely guarded secret, but there were two teapots always ready to use in response to the calls from the shop where I was billeted. One of them was a very large pot made of metal that was frequently topped up with boiling water from the urn which stood on the coal-fired kitchen range. Less often a few spoonfuls of tea leaves would be thrown in to strengthen the contents.

If the call was simply 'One tea with sugar!' the cup would be filled from the big teapot, although even that could soon be emptied if an Army lorry carrying lots of soldiers stopped outside the shop and they all came in wanting refreshments. But if the call included the name of the customer, a much smaller teapot was used. Invariably it would first be emptied, fresh tea leaves would be tossed in and boiling water from a small kettle poured over them. The contents were carefully stirred and then the cup was filled through a tea strainer.

One of the many special calls would be 'cup of tea for Mr Whitehead', who would usually have been seen driving down from the railway station in a small yellow van. Mr Whitehead was the head gardener at Parham House, the stately home of the Honourable Clive and Mrs Pearson. Yellow was the colour of the paint used on all of the

Parham estate vehicles and many other items, such as the entrance gates, cottage windows and doors and farm equipment.

During the war the beautiful walled gardens of Parham House were ploughed up, all the perennial flowering plants and herbaceous borders were removed and the land could only be used for growing vegetables. One of Mr Whitehead's regular jobs was to take boxes of produce to Pulborough Station to be loaded onto a London train. After doing that he needed a cup of tea before driving back to Parham.

Parham House and the Pearsons were often talked about in the shop, always in reverential tones. In the early part of the war the talk was about how they had taken in thirty evacuee children from Peckham to be billeted with them. People often wondered how the staff at Parham was managing to cope with them and how children from Peckham could find it possible to adjust to such totally different surroundings to the ones they had come from. I was quite jealous of the boys who had been selected to be billeted at Parham and wondered why I hadn't been so lucky, especially when I heard that Mrs Pearson had arranged for every one of them to be fitted by the local tailor for new suits soon after they arrived.

What Mr Whitehead felt when ordered by the Hon. Clive Pearson to divide up one of the borders in the ancient walled garden into small plots, one for each of the evacuees so that they could be taught how to grow salads and vegetables, is not known. However I heard that this was done, the theory being that if the boys had grown the vegetables themselves they would more readily eat them when they were cooked and served to them at mealtimes. Apparently the scheme was a great success, once the boys had been taught not to keep digging up the seeds to see if they were growing.

It must have been a great shock to the boys' parents when they made their first visit and saw the beautiful mansion set in its parklands, with the rolling hills of the South Downs in the background. Back home in crowded Peckham there were still a few traces of the days when it had been just a small village in rural Surrey on the borders of Kent. Its great days of glory were when wealthy people had carved small estates out of its fields and built large houses in which they could live in style, but still be within easy reach of central London.

When the railways came in 1826 it became possible to catch a train at Peckham Rye Station and arrive in the City a mere fifteen minutes later. As a result, Peckham and its surrounding area was rapidly developed to house the thousands of people who could now leave the congestion of old London, but still easily reach their places of employment. The days of commuting to work had arrived.

The owners of estates in rural Peckham cashed in on the demand for building sites and sold out to the developers. Most of their mansions were demolished, leaving only a few street names as mementoes of the area's former glory, names such as Lemon Road, which is all that is left of Basing Manor House where Sir Thomas Gardyner lived during the reign of King Charles I. He grew melons in his hothouses to present to the king. A few of the big houses did survive, but terraces of Victorian houses crowded right up to their doors. It is doubtful whether there was ever anything in the Peckham area to compare with the beauty of Parham.

Sadly the threat of invasion in 1940 brought an end to the stay of evacuees at Parham. The house and its parklands were commandeered by the Army, leaving just one wing for the Pearsons to live in. Nissen huts and concrete roadways were built in the park, and the Great Hall, with its connecting rooms, echoed to the noise of Army boots and shouted orders.

Today the soldiers have long since gone. Parham has been restored to its former glory and thousands of visitors now pass through its entrance gates and gasp with wonder when they get their first glimpse of the beautiful Elizabethan mansion. As they proceed in their cars and coaches they may perhaps notice the few concrete roadways that still lead off from the main drive into the wooded areas where hundreds of Canadian soldiers were based, ready to fight for England had the invaders come.

Today most of the signs of war have gone. The gardens are restored and many years have passed since Mr Whitehead used to drive to

Pulborough Station in the estate's yellow van, stopping off for a cup of tea at Burchell's shop, where I was probably hiding behind the sweet jars listening to every word that was said. But Parham has never forgotten its evacuees and has held several reunion events for them. The items they made during their stay at Parham are proudly displayed to visitors, along with the many other treasures. Lady Emma Barnard, who is a direct descendant of the late Hon. Clive and Mrs Pearson, resides at Parham with her husband James and two sons, and is a Patron of the Evacuees Reunion Association.

13

READY TO DO BATTLE

If during the Second World War the enemy forces had succeeded in effecting a landing on the south coast of England and in breaking out of their beachhead, it was realised that they would attempt to make a Panzer tank drive towards London, a mere sixty miles away. To prevent them reaching their target, various stop lines were created, one of them encompassing Pulborough, but of course those defences had to be tested, as did the ability of the troops, with the help of the Home Guard to 'hold the line'.

Strong forces of the Canadian Army were stationed throughout West Sussex, many in and around Pulborough, but the overall Commander-in-Chief of the region's defences was British. His headquarters were located at Lancing, near Worthing, from which orders were issued that on a certain weekend the stop line at Pulborough was to be tested. Units of the Canadian Army were to advance from the coast, acting as though they were the enemy. After breaking away from the seafront they were to overpower the defence of Arundel and then proceed at speed along the A29, across the Arun Valley to advance on Pulborough and capture it after defeating the local defence force, made up of other Canadian soldiers supported by the Home Guard.

The Swan Hotel was commandeered for the weekend and all its letting rooms had to be vacated for the use of the supervisory officers, with the ordinary soldiers camped under canvas in nearby fields. Lorries containing hundreds of small bags of powdered chalk taken from the South Downs were sent to Pulborough and stacked in various buildings around Swan Corner.

During the week prior to the 'battle', although it was supposed to be top secret, I heard that it was to take place on the Sunday, which everyone else also seemed to know. I duly went to see the fun and arrived to see the first of the 'enemy' tanks racing along the Causeway towards the two Swan bridges over the River Arun. Both of them had their steel tank barriers in place and members of the attacking troops were already struggling to remove them. At last they succeeded and the first of their tanks advanced to Swan Corner, only to be bombarded with bags of chalk from the roof and upper windows of the Swan Hotel and other roadside buildings. The bags of chalk represented hand grenades and shells. If one landed on a tank it had to immediately grind to a halt and be considered out of action. If a bag of chalk hit a foot soldier he was declared to be either dead or badly wounded and had to lie down at the side of the road.

The scene was one of complete chaos, but was very exciting to me and the other boys who had gathered there, not that we were allowed to stand where all the action was taking place. However during the height of the mock battle I had the great satisfaction of seeing one of Pulborough's most highly secret machine-gun posts in action. When I tell people about it now they laugh and think I have made the story up after watching episodes of *Dad's Army*. However they are wrong, because this is yet another of the many thousands of things that happened during the Second World War which now seem to be highly improbable.

One of the businesses that used to exist at Swan Corner was a motor repair company which traded under the name of Dreadnought Garage – why it was called that I have no idea. The workshops were housed in a collection of buildings, some built of corrugated-iron sheets on a wooden frame, but one was an ancient, stone-built former granary that fronted the main road. Across the front of that building the owners of the business had, many years before the war, fixed a large enamelled sign bearing the words 'Dreadnought Garage', behind which was a small window set into the thick stone wall.

On a few occasions a friend of ours, who was the son of the manager of the garage, would take us into the various buildings. On one such visit it was to see the fuselage of an RAF fighter plane that had recently been stored there. This was during the very early part of the war. He told us that it was highly secret and that we must not tell anyone what we had seen. However, we already knew of another that was stored in the garage of the Railway Hotel. I never did find out the story of those planes and can only assume that they were later taken away during the Battle of Britain to replace ones that had been shot down. Perhaps they were taken to the famous fighter station at Tangmere, where their wings would have been fitted. I may even have seen them in action in the many dogfights which took place over West Sussex.

Later we were shown another secret inside the workshops of the garage. It was a fully equipped machine-gun post built on the first floor, immediately behind the window that had been covered over by the enamel name sign. Our friend told us that part of the sign could be swivelled to one side, so enabling the machine gun to fire through the gap. The thickness of the old stone walls would have protected the gun crew from returned fire.

On the day of the mock battle I could see the gap in the sign and hear the sound of blanks being fired from the machine gun inside the building. It was the letter 'o' in 'Dreadnought' that could be swivelled to one side. Pure *Dad's Army* it may have been, but I feel sure that Captain Mainwaring would have thoroughly approved.

At about midday the mock battle seemed to be over and the men who were lying in the road covered in chalk dust pretending to be dead stood up, dusted themselves down and made their way to the bars of the Swan Hotel, which were now open for the two-hour session which was all that was legally allowed in those days. By good fortune, or perhaps due to special arrangements made between the Army and Tamplins Brewery, the Swan had ample stocks of beer that weekend in spite of the general shortage.

Not much now appeared to be happening so we boys all drifted away, me to my billet at the shop in time for Sunday dinner. Later I went back to Swan Corner to find that the soldiers, tanks, bren-gun carriers and Army lorries had all gone, leaving the men of the Home Guard to sweep up all the chalk from the roads and footpaths. I looked to see whether the 'o' in the Dreadnought Garage sign had been closed. It had, and was probably never opened again.

For days after the mock battle I wondered which side had supposedly won, but nobody seemed to know. However I did hear that the Commander-in-Chief had been in the Swan Hotel throughout the battle, watching from an upstairs window and that his verdict about the day was that it had all been 'A bloody shambles'. The name of that commanding officer was said to be none other than Bernard Montgomery, who very soon after was directed by Winston Churchill to go to North Africa and take command of the British Eighth Army and to drive the German and Italian forces into the sea which, as everyone knows, he duly did.

After that famous victory at El Alamein the tide began to turn against Hitler's Nazi Germany, his plans to invade Britain were eventually abandoned and the West Sussex stop line was never put to a real test.

However, another battle did take place at Pulborough a couple of years later. During the winter of 1942 there was a very heavy snowfall and a prolonged cold spell. All the roads were covered by a sheet of ice and many of the footpaths were deep in snow. In those times heavy snowfalls were commonplace during every winter in Sussex, but unlike present times the local authorities did very little to clear the roads. Petrol and diesel was in such short supply that salt spreaders could not be used. The most that one could expect was for the local road sweeper to scatter some sand on the steepest hills, or perhaps at a few road junctions.

Of course, only a few people owned a car and most of them had been laid up for the duration of the war. The few drivers who had been classed as essential workers did manage to get a very limited petrol ration and they all had sets of chains that could be fitted to their car wheels when snow had fallen and the roads were icy.

One of the evacuated teachers, Miss Dell of the Peckham Girls Central School, was billeted several miles out of the village and had been awarded a petrol ration. She owned what I believe was a very ancient Ford car; it was very small and looked rather like a black box on wheels trundling along. Every morning we would see her driving through the village on her way to the village hall school. She had no chains for the wheels and probably would have had no idea how to fit them even if she had bought a set.

As we watched her drive past, she would have thought it to be most improper to stop and offer us a lift; we waited to see the fun and were rarely disappointed. Virtually every day her little car would suddenly spin round as it hit a particularly icy stretch of the road. Miss Dell's reaction was equally predictable: she would brake hard, sometimes causing the car to spin even faster. Then we would run to her rescue and push the car so that it was again facing the right way and off she would go once more.

When she reached the village hall she persisted in parking her car on the slope from the road down to the front entrance, only to find she couldn't get it back up again when it was time to leave in the afternoon. The men who worked at the builders' yard opposite would come over and push sacking under her car wheels whilst shouting instructions. It was to be hoped that she never heard the things those men said about her, but even if she did the same performance was repeated every day until the thaw came.

The deep snow brought a fresh outburst of hostility between the evacuees and the village boys. They thought it was great fun to throw snowballs at the evacuee girls and try to knock their school hats off.

Whilst we evacuee boys felt it was alright for us to do that, we objected strongly to the village boys doing it. The inevitable result was that running snowball fights took place daily all along the main street of the village and several grown ups were hit, to their understandable annoyance.

That led to complaints being made to the head teacher of the village school and the head of the evacuees' school. We were all duly lectured, but still the snowball fights continued. Therefore the teachers of both schools met to decide what to do. They hit upon a plan to hold an organised snow fight between the boys of both schools in the recreation ground behind the village hall. On the appointed day we evacuees attending the village hall school were led outside and told to form up in a straight line. Then the village boys arrived and were made to form up in a line facing us, all the while shouting threats and insults at us, such as, 'You dirty Londoners, we're going to get you now!' I don't remember what we shouted back, but perhaps that's just as well.

One of the teachers called us all to order and said, 'You must all remain standing in your rows. When I blow my whistle you may begin to throw snowballs at each other, when I blow it again you must stop and stand still!' She duly blew her whistle and immediately the village boys charged forward, but we were ready for them and within seconds the scene was one of total mayhem, with boys being pushed over and rolled in the snow, some even being buried in it.

This was no friendly snow fight; this was a war of attrition in which old scores would be settled. The teachers attempted to restore order, but realising that no notice was being taken by us boys they retired to a safe distance. Gradually we became exhausted and the battle petered out. The teachers blew their whistles and declared the outcome to be a draw. The village boys went back to their homes and we went to our billets.

When I arrived at mine my foster mother took one look at me and said, 'Look at the state of you. Your clothes are wet through and your shirt is torn. What on earth have you been up to?' I think all the boys experienced the same reaction when they arrived indoors. Several people complained to the schools, saying that the teachers should have known better.

However the unexpected outcome was that no more snowballs were thrown, for the simple reason that the next morning our arms ached so much we could hardly lift them, let alone throw a snowball. By the time we had recovered a thaw had set in and soon all the snow had melted away. I think that the snow battle also, at last, brought an end to the hostility between the village boys and we evacuees.

The thaw inevitably resulted in the River Arun overtopping its banks and flooding the surrounding fields known as the Brooks. After a few sharp night frosts the flood waters froze over and crowds of people, especially those who possessed ice skates, would have great fun. While the Canadian soldiers were stationed at Pulborough they would join in, many of them being very accomplished skaters and willing to teach us how to do it. Many long-standing friendships were formed, some of them led to marriages and to some Sussex girls emigrating to Canada to join their husbands when the war finally ended.

14

DAYS AND HAPPENINGS THAT MAKE MEMORIES

I am one of those people who have a very good memory, at least in respect of things that happened to me many years ago and especially during the years I spent as an evacuated schoolboy in West Sussex. However if you ask me what I was doing or may have said only a few weeks ago, my response will probably be hesitant and vague.

In previous chapters of the book I have recounted some of the major events in which as a schoolboy I was either involved in or witnessed, but there are several minor happenings that were less important but will never be forgotten, at least not by me.

One of them relates to an event that took place very early in the war, while I was still attending the village school at Pulborough. News had spread that there was a national epidemic of the then dreaded disease called diphtheria and that many children throughout the country were said to have died from it. Nowadays children are immunised against it during the first years of their lives, but in 1939/40 such precautions were still rare.

In common with all young boys I believed the many scary stories that were told about diphtheria and repeated them to anyone who would listen, adding to the horrors with each telling. I firmly believed that if you caught that disease it would kill you within a few days.

The then Ministry of Health decided that immediate action had to be taken to prevent the illness really becoming a national problem. Orders were issued that all schoolchildren should be immunised. However that could only be carried out with the written consent of the parents. In normal times the procedure was simple – the schools would be supplied with printed consent forms to be issued to parents for them to sign and return to the school. But in the reception areas there were now thousands of children who were no longer in daily contact with their parents, making it very difficult to obtain written consents. Just how that problem was overcome I do not know. Perhaps the foster parents were authorised to decide upon such things by a form of proxy.

Whatever the legal position may have been I do know that one morning at school all we evacuees were lined up and marched through the village to a building known as the Church Men's Club, which was a wooden structure standing on a plot of land just off Lower Street. Waiting there for us was a man wearing a long white coat, who I believe was a doctor. The district nurse was also in attendance. We were all told to take off our jackets and roll up the left sleeve of our shirts. A needle was jabbed into the arm of each boy and after a quick dab with cotton wool smelling of antiseptic we put our jackets back on and walked back to school to continue our lessons. No fuss, no bother, but course when the local boys asked us what had happened and whether it hurt we exaggerated, telling them it was very, very painful and that there was blood all over the floor. Naturally that made them very apprehensive and fearful about what would happen to them when it was their turn to be vaccinated the next day.

Imagine our delight the following morning when they all arrived at the school with their mothers, who were to go with them to the Church Men's Club. Of course, we told them that they were all babies or cissies and that we hadn't needed to have our mothers there to hold our hands. Later, to our great delight, we heard that one of the village boys who had constantly tried to bully us had fainted as soon as the doctor went to inoculate him. That truly was a great day for we evacuees.

Another of my memories is of something I did that had to be kept strictly secret to avoid me being in serious trouble. At the shop they had what was called a Vantas drinks machine, which could make cold fizzy drinks of various flavours. It had several levers: one squirted a measure of concentrated liquid into a drinking glass, another topped it up with clear water and finally a shot of gas was injected from a cylinder that stood beside the machine. The resulting glass of fizzy drink was then sold to the customer, probably for 1d.

So far so good, but it became one of my many jobs to make up the bottles of concentrated flavoured liquid. That job was always done on the bench of a large dresser which stood in the scullery behind the main living room, which usually meant there was no one around to keep an eye on what I was doing. The concentrated flavourings came in slabs, rather like bars of chocolate. My job was to break off a couple of long pieces and push them into bottles, which I then filled with water, later giving them each a vigorous shake.

One day I decided to break off a piece of the flavouring and eat it, which resulted in less going into the bottle. It didn't really taste very nice, but I persevered and as a result the final drinks were rather weaker than they should have been. This became the normal procedure for me, although I did have an anxious moment on one particularly hot day when a customer came in and asked for a glass of Vantas orangeade. That was made for him, with the usual clunking and hissing noises from the machine as the various levers were pulled and the gas tap turned on.

The customer took a drink from his glass and immediately complained, saying it was very weak. Of course it was; the orange flavouring was my favourite, so I had probably taken a big bite out of the concentrated bar. I quickly hurried way from my place behind the sweet jars, expecting to hear my foster father shouting for me, but to my great relief he said to the customer, 'Yes I know! All the flavours seem to be weaker now. I suppose it's due to the war and they can't get the ingredients at the factory.' I could breathe again – my secret had not been discovered! I never did hear whether my foster father ever found out that I was really the culprit. If he didn't it's far too late now!

My next tale from those days involves chickens' eggs. As I have mentioned before, my foster father kept quite a lot of chickens. The garden behind the shop was very small, so he rented some land beyond the railway station where he had set up chicken houses and wire netting runs. When I first went to live with the Burchells their shop was not as busy as it became when all the soldiers arrived in the area.

Their daughter, Gwen, who had fairly recently left school, worked in the shop and served in the tearoom which had been built alongside. Gwen became my great friend and still is to this day. I referred to her as my foster sister and still do. Every afternoon someone had to go to the chicken runs to check that everything was in order and to collect the eggs, which were then carried back to the shop in a deep wicker basket. Often Gwen would do that job and I would go with her. One day she showed me how she could swing the wicker basket over her head without any of the eggs falling out and being broken. I was really impressed.

As the war developed the shop became much busier and Gwen could not be spared to attend to the chickens, so that job became mine. Of course I tried to copy the basket swinging trick but failed miserably, several of the eggs falling to the ground and smashing. Nothing was said when I got back to the shop and I thought I had got away with it, so the next day I tried again, only to smash even more eggs this time. When I got back to the shop my foster father was waiting for me and looked straight into the basket, then at me, saying, 'Not many eggs again today! Do you know why?' I mumbled that I didn't know why, to which he said, 'Well I do! Someone saw you swinging the basket over your head and told me about it. Don't ever try doing that again!'

While this was going on Gwen was standing nearby looking very anxious, but I didn't 'split' on her. I never did find out who had told my foster father about my basket-swinging attempts.

Another of the family chores that I used to do with Gwen was to take flowers to the village churchyard to place on her grandparents' grave. In those days there was a shortcut across the recreation ground to a small gate that opened into the churchyard. To reach her grandparents' grave you passed by a rather unusual wooden memorial to the late Dr Spear, who I believe had been the village general practitioner for many years.

Gwen would always place a hand on the memorial and say, 'Dr Spear, I do feel queer, but not as queer as you I fear!' I used to copy her, but for this there were no consequences to worry about. No doubt she had learned that little saying from her father or her village friends. I believe that the worthy Dr Spear had died many years earlier.

My foster parents were very kindly and took great care of me, but they were strict, as was commonplace in those days. Every Sunday morning I had to wear my best suit, polish my shoes and walk to the village school where Bible lessons were held. Then it was back to my billet for Sunday dinner, after which I was supposed to go to another Sunday school held in the parish church. I hated both of those sessions and often played truant, once to watch the mock Army battle at Swan Corner.

Whether my truancy was ever discovered I don't know, but one day I thought all was lost. On that occasion I had an accomplice, my brother John, who was by then billeted elsewhere. Instead of going to a boring Sunday school lesson we set off for a walk along Steppey Lane and then started to follow a footpath that was new to us. We could still see the grey stone tower of the church and the hands of its big clock and realised that it was time for us to go back to our billets for Sunday dinner.

It was then that we realised that two huge carthorses were standing beside a wooden footbridge over a stream we had to cross. I don't know which of us was most scared of those horses, John or me. They showed no sign of moving away from the footbridge, so we decided to leap across the stream further along. John managed it alright but I finished up with one foot in the water. As we ran across the field to its gate both horses came galloping towards us. Fear does make you run faster and we both reached the gate and climbed over it before the horses caught up with us.

I still had the problem of one of my best shoes being full of water and coated with mud, plus a soaking wet woollen sock. As soon as I went indoors I was told to sit at the table because dinner was ready. That meant my wet sock and muddy shoe could not be seen and after dinner I went out again and managed to get things dry. Not an important happening I know, but it does show how things that would probably have been of little consequence at home became much more serious for an evacuee if discovered by one's foster parents, who may perhaps have been less tolerant of such little mishaps than our real parents.

I later discovered that those two carthorses were actually quite harmless and just loved being made a fuss of, which is why they ran towards us.

Did you know that the legs of chickens are nice and warm to hold, especially on a cold winter's day? Provided, of course, that the chickens had not had their necks wrung! Every so often my foster father would need my help to move egg-laying hens from one chicken run to another, so as to enable him, again with my help, to carefully scrape the perches of the now empty hen house and thoroughly scrub all the woodwork with strong disinfectant. This was to kill off any red mites that may be present; they are parasites that can cause great harm to chickens.

If you try to catch chickens during the day they are very elusive and will run around squawking, flapping their wings and becoming very distressed, which can cause them to stop laying eggs. However if you wait until dusk, when they have gone to roost for the night, you can simply lift them off their perches, holding them upside down by their legs, and carry them to their new hen house where they immediately settle on a perch and go back to sleep. They don't struggle to get free or make any noise, and on a cold winter's evening you have the added benefit of nice warm hands.

With the shop and the tearoom always so busy I was given more and more jobs to do, especially with regard to the chickens. Every afternoon I had to carry their heavy buckets of feeding stuff to put in their troughs. Of course the hens would always 'mob' me as I did that, but they never pecked me. However there was, for a while, an evil cockerel who would wait until my back was turned, then silently rush forward and peck the backs of my legs. It hurt, especially as, in common with all schoolboys at that time, I wore short trousers.

One day after he had pecked me, I ran after him with a stick. I wasn't going to hurt him, simply teach him a lesson. I was seen by one of the men working in an adjoining allotment and he told my foster father, who in turn gave me a telling off. When I tried to explain that the old cockerel kept pecking me he just laughed, telling me that I must be a big sissy to be bothered by an old cockerel.

A few days later I was helping my foster father to dig over the chicken run where the cockerel lived. I saw him lurking at the far end of the run, waiting for his chance to strike. My foster father was digging with his back to him, but I saw him start to run forward. 'The old cockerel's coming,' I warned, but my foster father simply muttered, 'So what!' Almost immediately the vicious cockerel reached him and promptly gave him a mighty peck on his backside. 'Yew owld bugger!' shouted by foster father, who then grabbed the bird and promptly wrung its neck. I resisted the urge to say, 'I told you so!' We ate the old cockerel for dinner the following Sunday.

As part of the war effort schoolchildren were expected to actively participate in a wide variety of campaigns, such as collecting stinging nettles, horse chestnuts (conkers), hips and haws, blackberries and many other such items. Very often we had little or no idea how certain things we collected could possibly help win the war, but that didn't deter us from joining in. However, the collection of sheep's wool to be used for making warm clothing for the airmen flying Spitfires and Hurricanes and for the crews of the RAF bombers that were hitting back at the enemy in the heart of Germany made immediate sense.

Wherever sheep were put to graze, their wool could be found on barbed-wire fences, hawthorn hedges and brambles. So off we would go with large carrier bags, determined to find as much wool as possible. Of course much of the wool we collected was very dirty, tangled and mixed up with twigs, grass and even bits of rusty barbed wire. So before it could be handed in at the collection post it had to be picked over to remove all the rubbish, which was not a pleasant job. Once when I was sorting through a bag of recovered wool I found, to my horror, pieces of dried skin and blood, which rather put me off wool collecting.

On an entirely different topic, I have memories of being invited to take tea, along with my brother and sister, with Miss Ambler, the rather formidable headmistress of the Peckham Central Girls' School. She had rented a large house standing in a well-maintained garden, where I believe she lived with her elderly mother whom she had brought with her when the school was evacuated to Pulborough.

Miss Ambler was determined to create and maintain good relations between her school and the people of Pulborough. To help with that she worked hard to instil into us evacuees the concept that we were, in effect, all ambassadors of London and that we should at all times conduct ourselves in such a way as to give the best possible impression to the local people. 'You are not from the inner-city slums, although many think that is the case!' she would tell us. 'Always act correctly and politely. Remember we are, in effect, the uninvited guests that they have taken into their homes and always behave accordingly.'

Just why me and my brother John were invited to tea remains a mystery, because although we had been evacuated with Miss Ambler's school we were not then her pupils. Perhaps it was due to our sister Jean, who was one of her 'star' pupils. Coping with the array of cutlery, napkins and ornate crockery presented no problems to me because our mother had taught us all that from an early age. However, some of the accents of the adult guests were rather different to mine and to that of most of the customers who gathered in my foster parents' shop. For example, I believe that Owld Frosty the parson was one of those present.

Perhaps Miss Ambler thought that because I was billeted in a busy shop I must be in contact with many of the local people and therefore in an ideal place to create a good impression. Little did she know about my secret listening post behind the display of sweet jars.

One day as I was walking to school, I noticed that great activity was taking place in the field behind the Swan Hotel. Dozens of Army lorries were parked in the field and tents were being set up for the soldiers to live in – another much larger one was to be their cookhouse and mess room. Everywhere there were stacks of steel sheets and girders. It all looked very important.

Someone told me that they were going to build another bridge over the River Arun, but I found that hard to believe because there were two bridges, standing side by side, already there. The oldest of them was no longer used for traffic; it had been built hundreds of years ago to replace a ferry, but was too narrow to cope with modern traffic. A new, much wider, bridge was built alongside it in the 1930s, so why, I wondered, was the Army going to built yet another one?

I soon found out that the bridge building was actually a training exercise. They were to erect what was called a Bailey bridge, many of which would be used by our troops during the invasion of France following D-Day! It was realised that the retreating Germans would blow up the existing bridges over rivers and canals in an attempt to halt, or at least delay, the advance of the Allies. Bailey bridges were prefabricated structures which could be erected very quickly.

Work started immediately on building the bridge over the River Arun and I believe the exercise was being carefully timed by a group of senior officers. The sections of the bridge had to be bolted together and the whole structure was then pushed into place across the river. At least that was the theory, but we saw that there was a tank on the opposite bank pulling the bridge over the water. Would that have been possible in a real war situation, we wondered.

As soon as the Bailey bridge had been properly secured a continuous stream of tanks, bren-gun carriers, Army lorries, jeeps and staff cars trundled over it, then joined the main road over the permanent bridge, back into the Swan Hotel field and repeated the circle time and time again. A few days later the exercise was over, the bridge was dismantled and all signs of the Army had gone. I often wonder whether that Bailey bridge was ever used in a real war situation.

Among many memories of my years in wartime Sussex are those of the tiny hamlet of Stopham, which is actually some distance from the famous bridge of that name. In fact, to find it you have to leave the main road and go along a 'no through' lane which brings you to a cluster of stone-built cottages and a tiny church which dates from the eleventh century.

Stopham Church is a place I have always loved to visit. As soon as you enter its porch and push open its heavy oak door you feel its centuries-old atmosphere. Everywhere you look there are memorials to the Barttelot family, who came to England with William the Conqueror. One of them married the heiress of Stopham in 1428 and their descendants still live in the parish. Throughout the centuries, members of the Barttelot family have served in British military campaigns throughout the world and the standards of their various regiments, some now faded and tattered due to their great age, hang from the walls of this ancient church and their names can be seen on many memorials.

During the Second World War the Kingsley School of Croydon was evacuated to Stopham. The children travelled by train from Croydon to Pulborough, where they changed on to a steam train that would take them along the branch line to the first station, that of Fittleworth. From there they went along the lane to Stopham, where they were welcomed by the rector, the Revd W.B. Masefield (who later lost his life when a stray German plane dropped a bomb that fell on the road to Pulborough as he was passing in his car).

The tiny school at Stopham had been closed for many years but was reopened for the Croydon children to use. During the following December a Christmas party was held for the evacuees at

Stopham House, where Sir Walter Barttelot played Father Christmas. Many years have passed since those children from Croydon were evacuated to the tiny hamlet of Stopham. Those who have survived will now be in their retirement years, but I am sure they have never forgotten the time they spent all those years ago in such a delightful part of Sussex.

15

LET'S GO TO THE SEASIDE!

The threat of invasion had passed, the sun was shining every day, it was summertime and we were on holiday. In peacetime we would all have gone away, at least for a few days, perhaps to the seaside, but due to the war that had not been possible for several years. Gwen, my foster sister as I called her because she was just like a big sister to me, decided that on the following Wednesday, which was early closing day for the shop, we would go the Sussex seaside town of Littlehampton.

According to our friend the goods porter, if we caught the 1.28 p.m. train from Pulborough Station we would arrive at Littlehampton by 2.30 p.m., and to come back we should catch the 6.43 p.m. from Littlehampton, which was a fast train that got us back to Pulborough at 7.21 p.m. The shop closed at midday, leaving us with plenty of time to have some lunch before walking up to the station. One or two of Gwen's friends were to join us on our trip to the seaside.

We all thought we would be enjoying Littlehampton's fine sandy beach, so we had with us our bathing trunks, costumes and towels, and also a bucket and spade that Gwen had kept since before the war. Gwen's mother had made sandwiches filled with egg or fish paste – even though they ran a shop many food items were simply unobtainable, especially ham and cheese.

During the train journey I was told to look out for various places and buildings of interest. As a small boy I was always glued to a window during every train, bus or car journey I made and was determined not to miss anything. In fact, that is something I still do and find it strange that today's children seem to take little interest in the passing scenery.

One of the things I was told to look out for was Amberley Castle, a romantic, grey stone building complete with towers, battlements and a drawbridge. Just a little further on the railway ran past what is now the Amberley Chalk Works Museum, but during the war was still working as a commercial company producing lime for use on the fields. Nearby in a cutting off the River Arun could be seen some wooden barges that used to carry chalk and lime upriver to Pulborough and downstream to the port of Littlehampton.

The next station after Amberley was that of Arundel, where a castle that is the historic home of the Dukes of Norfolk towers over the little town. The River Arun here is much wider and very fast flowing according to the tide. Soon we arrived at Littlehampton, where the railway terminates. The station is situated some distance from the seaside, so we set off walking to get, as we thought, to the beach as quickly as possible, not realising that a great disappointment awaited us.

To our dismay we found that the coast road was permanently closed to all traffic and pedestrians and we only got a glimpse of the sea through many coils of barbed wire that lined the beach. Big notices said, 'Danger. Do not enter!' A soldier told us that the beach was mined and as I looked around I could see lots of machine gun posts and gun emplacements. Littlehampton beach was seen as a likely place for the Germans to land if they had attempted to invade England. I was told years later that Littlehampton beach was one of the places where pipelines were laid that could pump blazing oil out to sea to burn any invading Army boats and men. Whether that is factually true or not I do not know.

Rather disconsolately we wandered back into the town, passing what in peacetime had been a big funfair. One or two of the stalls

The Sands, Littlehampton.

East Beach, 1930s. (Image supplied by Littlehampton Museum)

were open and there were even some dodgem cars running, but most of the site was boarded up and looked derelict. Gwen told me that the funfair belonged to the man who founded the famous Butlin's holiday camps. She said that there was a big one at Bognor Regis, just along the coast, but that it had been commandeered by the armed forces to use as a barracks.

The road into town took us beside the River Arun, which was quite wide at this point before joining the sea. There were crowds of people wandering about. They had probably all thought, like us, that they would have been able to spend a few hours on the beach. Then we saw that a long queue of people had formed to take their turn to be ferried across the river to the opposite bank, which actually had a narrow strip of sand at the water's edge. It was hardly a sandy beach, but it was better than nothing.

It looked very crowded on that little 'beach', but people were wading and swimming in the water so we decided to join the queue and after a long wait it was our turn to clamber aboard the ferry boat, which in fact was only a wide, open-topped wooden boat fitted with plank seats. It had no engine and had to be rowed across the river by an elderly man. He packed as many people on board as he dared, cast off and started rowing hard. The tide was running out very fast, but he got us safely across and tied the boat up at a small landing stage. I believe the fare was 6d for adults and 3d for children. We eventually found a space to sit on the little beach where we could eat our sandwiches and change into our bathing things for a paddle, but the water was rather muddy and it was not safe to go in very deep due to the fast-flowing current.

All too soon it was time to pack up our things, queue again for the ferry boat and make our way to the railway station. So much for our day at the seaside!

Undeterred, Gwen later persuaded her parents that we should go by bus to Brighton, where she wanted to buy some new clothes, probably from one of the big stores such as Marks & Spencer or British Home Stores. Of course, Pulborough had no shops to compare with them. She had carefully checked her clothing coupons book and mine, persuading me that I didn't need all of my coupons, and with them she should be able to get what she wanted. Perhaps as a way of getting me to give up some of my coupons she promised that we would go to a theatre.

The journey to Brighton was an easy one, because the Southdown Bus Co. ran a regular service that stopped outside the shop at Pulborough, where the drivers and conductors called in for their cups of tea. Of course we still had to pay our bus fares and make sure we had our identity cards with us ready to show to the police or military people if required.

Eventually the day came for our visit to Brighton and as soon as the bus arrived we got on and tried to get a seat on the top deck, right at the front. That was at my insistence because I wanted a good view on the journey. Due to the overcrowding on all the buses at that time, finding a seat, any seat, was difficult. The bus was already packed with soldiers, and in fact the Southdown Bus Co. often used to run two buses together in an attempt to cope with all the passengers. Every seat on our bus appeared to be taken already, but the Canadian soldiers kindly made room for us by sitting on the floor. Of course Gwen came in for a lot of teasing from the soldiers, some saying, 'You can sit on my lap if you like!' It was all in fun and she was used to all that sort of thing from the many soldiers who came into the shop. Some of them got off the bus at the gates to Parham Park where they had a hutted camp, so that made things less crowded.

On the journey the bus took us past Shoreham Aerodrome, which was by then an RAF base, where I saw some Spitfires on the ground. Lancing College, high on the South Downs, was pointed out to me and I was told it was being used as the Army's Southern Command Headquarters.

Eventually we reached the bus terminus at Brighton and made our way to the big shops. Gwen kept a tight hold on me, but I think she was more afraid of getting lost than me; after all, I was born in London and had been used to crowded streets and big stores before being evacuated. After Gwen had found the items she wanted, or been told that they were not available due to the war or that she hadn't got enough clothing coupons, we went for a walk along the seafront.

Of course, as at Littlehampton, the beach was securely closed to the public. Both the Palace Pier and the West Pier had had their middle sections blown up to prevent them being used by the enemy as landing stages. On the promenade were several structures that had been made to look like ice-cream kiosks, but were actually gun emplacements. The beach was festooned with barbed wire and lines of posts which were there to wreck or capsize any landing craft and could be seen at low tide.

As we walked through the town centre I saw a few bomb-damaged and boarded-up shops, but nothing on the scale that I had seen in London during my brief visits home. We found the theatre where our seats had been booked for a matinée performance. All that I can remember is that it was a variety show, but I have no idea who appeared in it. Then it was time to catch our bus and return to dear old Pulborough.

I don't recall any other visits to the seaside during my evacuation years, but that is not surprising because all the beaches were closed and there was always too much work to do, much of it connected with the war effort.

16

KEEPING IN TOUCH WITH HOME

It always comes as a surprise when we former evacuees tell people today that we did not know where we were being taken to on evacuation day. They become even more incredulous when we add that our parents didn't know either. In fact, the government insisted that great secrecy regarding the whole operation should be observed. So when the long crocodile files of children were being led from their schools in London, Manchester, Leeds, Sheffield, Liverpool, Birkenhead, Newcastle and the many other designated evacuation areas, all their parents could do was to watch in grim-faced silence. At most places they were not allowed to walk with us, or to go into the railway stations to wave us off. Later on the day of departure they would find that a handwritten notice had been hung on the school gates, saying, 'This school has been evacuated to .... and is now closed'. At my sister's school the notice read, 'This school has been evacuated to Pulborough, West Sussex'.

So at least our parents had some idea where we now were, but they still didn't know who we were living with or how they could contact us. To overcome that problem the government had instructed the schools to issue us all with a pre-stamped postcard, already bearing our parents' names and address. During the days prior to evacuation, when the signal to 'Evacuate Forthwith' had still not been issued by the government, younger children, including me, were told what we should write on our postcard after getting our foster parents to enter their names and address. In my mind's eye I can still see the blackboard on which the words that we were to write on our cards were given in big letters. They were, 'Dear Mum and Dad, I am living with very nice people. I like it here and am very happy. Don't worry about me.' The postcard was then to be sent off straight away.

Nowadays I often give talks about the evacuation to schoolchildren. Mostly they listen with great interest and a lot of incredulity. I was rather taken aback at one school when a girl put her hand up and said, 'Why didn't you use your mobiles?' It seems incredible now, but in 1939 very few private houses had a telephone – my parents certainly didn't and neither did my foster parents. Urgent messages could be sent by telegram and most letters would arrive at their destination the day after posting. Many years were to pass before mobile phones were invented!

Soon after I arrived at my billet near Pulborough, I wrote my postcard home and took it to the postbox just down the lane. Years later my mother reminded me what I had had actually written, which was: 'Dear Mum and Dad. We have lost John and the stinging nettles got me on the way to the hut they call the lavatory!' Fortunately I was with my sister, who would have sent a much more reassuring message; well, she was five years older than me.

We were then given strict orders by our teachers that we must send a letter home every week. Our foster parents were also instructed to ensure that we did, but they were also told to read every letter before it was posted and if an evacuee had included words such as, 'Please Mummy, I want to come home' or 'I am very unhappy. Let me come home', they were to make their evacuees rewrite their letter, deleting such words. Many evacuees' letters were never even posted.

In an earlier chapter I have described the first visit our parents made to us after evacuation day. During the period known as the Phoney War they tried to come and see us once a month, but once the Blitz started that became very difficult. Train services were often badly disrupted, or cancelled altogether due to bomb damage on the lines. Even the companies running the 'Visit the Evacuees' special coaches had great difficulty in maintaining the service due to enemy action, such as bomb-damaged roads, unexploded bombs, blazing fires and even direct hits on their garages. We saw less and less of our father because he was either working seven days a week in the London docks or was on Home Guard duty.

I remember a visit our mother made to us at the height of the Blitz. She had not been to bed for weeks and night after night the sirens had sounded, the bombers came over and all that could be heard was the 'throb, throb, throb' of their engines, the crump of bombs falling, the deafening noise of the anti-aircraft guns and the bells of the ambulances and fire engines (they were not fitted with sirens in those days). When her train finally arrived at Pulborough Station about an hour later, I realised how tired she was. After calling at the shop to visit my foster parents she then went on to Ferrymead, where my brother John was billeted.

She didn't talk very much about the bombing; in fact, she was too exhausted to do very much at all. John's foster mother made her very welcome and persuaded her to stay at Pulborough for a couple of nights so that she could have a good rest. Somehow they must have got a message through to our father telling him that she was staying away for a night or two. The rest did her a power of good and soon she was back to her normal self.

For the first two years of the war there was no possibility of me going home to London to spend Christmas with my family as it was considered far too dangerous. I was bitterly disappointed in 1940, but my parents' concern was more than justified because on 30 December 1940 London was subjected to its most devastating raid. Some 136 enemy planes dropped over 22,000 fire bombs on the City of London area. The resulting fires were greater than those of the Great Fire of London in 1666. Over 20,000 firemen fought the blaze.

Above the blazing inferno St Paul's Cathedral stood defiant. Watching from near 10 Downing Street Winston Churchill issued the order to 'Save St Paul's at all costs!' It was saved and became London's beacon of hope and people would say, 'While St Paul's stands we will win the war!' From outside my parents' house you could look over London and see the dome of St Paul's. Every morning after a heavy raid during the night, my father would look to see if St Paul's had survived and gave a cheer when he saw it still proudly standing.

Much later in the war when the V1 flying bombs and the V2 rockets were raining down on London, I was already at home and I used to follow my father's example, little knowing that in 2009 I would be organising a commemorative service in that famous building to mark the seventieth anniversary of the great evacuation of British children during the Second World War. It would be attended by over 2,000 former evacuees and their families, many of them travelling from as far as New Zealand, Australia, Canada and the United States of America to be present.

In the summer of 1941 it was agreed that John and I could return home for a short holiday. We were both wildly excited and found it hard to wait for the day when we would say goodbye to Sussex for a few days and board the train that would take us to our real home. Gwen walked up to the station with us, and our friend the goods porter carried our things under the subway to the 'up' platform and saw us safely into a compartment, then without us knowing had a word with the guard to 'Keep an eye on us!'

As usual I grabbed a window seat and looked out onto the passing countryside and at the ever-increasing number of houses as we drew nearer to London. But first came Horsham, then the strange-sounding Three Bridges, followed by Gatwick, which was then just a narrow, grass-grown platform alongside an airfield with a few Nissen huts and one or two RAF fighter planes. The sign on the platform bore the words 'Gatwick Halt'. How very different that area is now!

My excitement grew as I began to see red buses and I knew that soon we would be arriving at Victoria Station, our terminus.

Our mother would be waiting for us at the ticket barrier and so too would be one of our uncles who was a member of the railway police and would be wearing his uniform. Then we boarded a bus or tram and made our way to Camberwell. Already I could see how battered London had become due to the bombing. There were gaps where whole buildings had been destroyed; others were shored up to stop them from collapsing. Many shops were boarded up and most had lost their big windows.

Arriving at Shenley Road, where our real home was, I saw a gap which had been created by a bomb in the long row of Victorian bay-fronted houses. Most houses had their windows blown in by bomb blasts and were now covered with black rubber like roofing felt, which could be collected from the nearest council depot together with wooden battens and nails. Everywhere looked very dirty and run down. Our house was still intact, but most of its ornate ceilings had fallen down and doors no longer fitted due to bomb blasts, but it was still that great place which we knew as home.

Jean, our sister, was already back in London, having reached school-leaving age and therefore was no longer an evacuee. Once an evacuee reached school-leaving age the government was no longer interested in you, or whether you stayed in the country or went home. Either way you had to get a job and earn enough money to pay for your board and keep and all your living costs. The government would not again be interested in you until you reached the age of eighteen and were therefore liable to a 'call up' to serve in the armed forces.

Ernest, another of our brothers, was also at home but still at school. He had been evacuated but when our mother visited him she found he was not being properly looked after and was in very poor health, so she promptly took him home and nursed him better. Ted, our eldest brother, was in the Army somewhere in North Africa.

Our brief stay at home ended all too soon and it was time to return to Pulborough, but not without tears being shed by both of us as the train pulled slowly out of Victoria Station.

There were several more such visits home. Each were so very welcome, but soon I found myself getting worried about things in Pulborough while I was away, concerning myself with such questions as: were my young lettuce plants being watered? Were they managing to look after the chickens if the shop was very busy? Little did I realise that slowly, perhaps imperceptibly, I was becoming a country boy, with all the responsibilities that entailed. I already spoke in a fairly strong Sussex accent. It seems that my Sussex roots were taking over my life. My mother was born in Robertsbridge in East Sussex, where my late grandfather had been the village carrier and kept a team of horses. Later he worked on the Kent & East Sussex Light Railway.

My father's family originated from a village in Kent, where they had worked on the land. I was born in London, but perhaps was not really a Londoner and most certainly not a Cockney. However, a few more years were to pass before I really discovered my true lifestyle.

17

You Can Come Home!

In common with the majority of evacuees, I yearned for the day when I could finally be allowed to return home for good. I would think back to the days before being evacuated, when I was part of a happy, united family. It was a life of total security and certainty of being really wanted no matter what I did or said. I sincerely believed that when I ceased to be an evacuee and went home, everything would be just the same and that homesickness would no more be a problem which had to be hidden and never talked about.

After Nazi Germany attacked Russia and the tide of war at last began to turn in favour of the Allies, the need for children to remain evacuated in this country ceased to be seen as necessary. The number of evacuees in areas such as Sussex showed a rapid decrease, although that was primarily due to many of them reaching school-leaving age. In London the bombing had ceased and in Sussex the threat of invasion no longer existed.

It was in 1943 that, to my great delight, I received a letter from my parents saying they had decided that I could, at long last, return home. This was the news I had eagerly awaited for the past four years and I was wildly excited. I rushed around the village telling everyone my news, but on the actual day of leaving I experienced feelings of sadness, which I did not understand. 'I'll come back to see you,' I told everyone, little knowing just how true that would eventually become. On the train journey to London I felt strangely subdued and failed to become excited by the sight of red buses and trams.

Within days of returning to London I was missing Sussex. At home all I could see from my bedroom window were the backs of the houses in the next road, unlike at Pulborough where the view was of the South Downs. Another problem was the attitude of some of the people I met in London. I recall an occasion when I was out with my mother and she stopped to talk to a neighbour who pointed at me and asked, 'And who is this boy then?' My mother replied, 'Oh, he is my youngest son who has been an evacuee!' The neighbour looked at me and said, 'Oh you were one of the lucky ones. You were not really in the war, were you?' I was furious and replied, 'In Sussex we were being bombed and machine gunned before anything happened in London and we had to expect to be invaded!' My mother was very cross with me, saying, 'That was very rude. You mustn't speak to people like that.' But I was totally unrepentant.

Very soon I was expressing my total dislike of London and its way of life. In retrospect I realise I must have been a real pain to my parents and I feel guilty about the way I treated my mother. Ever since evacuation day in 1939 she must have yearned for the moment when her family would again be fully reunited. She probably remembered me as her little eight-year-old boy who used to go around the house singing, but he had gone forever and in his place had come a rather serious, self-reliant boy of twelve who made clear his dissatisfaction with his home and surroundings; who often would say that as soon as he could he would return to Sussex.

My parents made every effort to resettle me, but it was to no avail. They even managed to find a plot of land that I could use as an allotment, thinking that might help. It was actually a bomb site that I had to clear of rubble before trying to grow anything in the rather poor soil. I left school when I was fourteen and a job was found for me in the Royal Parks; to be precise it was in the Queen Mary's Rose

Gardens of Regents Park. Everyone thought I was so very lucky and that a good career in parks gardening had been made available to me. But that was not what I wanted – I wanted to be back in my beloved Sussex.

Within a couple of years I succeeded in gaining a job in a market garden near Pulborough and took lodgings with the people who had been my brother's foster parents. When I broke the news to my parents I expected there to be uproar, but instead their response was to say, 'Well, nothing we can say will stop you from returning to Sussex!'

I spent several happy years back in Pulborough before having again to leave; this time it was due to being called up for National Service in the Royal Air Force. Sadly the demands of marriage, children and employment prevented another return to Sussex, but not to rural life. For over thirty-five years I have lived in a tiny village in the heart of rural Nottinghamshire. Our cottage is over 300 years old and tall people have to duck to avoid the low beams of some of its rooms.

In the distance is a range of low hills with a clump of trees that could almost be a copy of Chanctonbury Ring. Sadly, dairy farming has virtually ceased in the area and arable farming is now highly mechanised. I frequently visit West Sussex and I am still in touch with Gwen, my former foster sister of the evacuation years. Of course Pulborough, in common with most rural areas, has changed dramatically, but get away from the A29 and other main roads and take a walk along the back lanes and there the Sussex that I remember with such great affection can still be found and enjoyed.

Other titles published by The History Press

A Schoolboy's War in Essex
DAVID F. WOOD

David F. Wood recalls his days as a schoolboy in Essex, where his family moved when the Luftwaffe threatened his native London. With the same sense of fascination that grips many men of his generation, he describes watching airmen parachute to safety during the Battle of Britain and witnessing a Messerschmitt dramatically crash-landing close to his home. The accounts of his days spent playing with his new friends in the nearby countryside provide a stark contrast to the ravages of a war that was going on all around them.

978 0 7524 5517 4

A Schoolboy's War in Cornwall
JIM REEVE

In this poignant book, the author shares vivid memories of his evacuation from war-torn London to the comparative safety of places like Newquay, St Ives and Redruth in Cornwall. From touching recollections of enjoyable days spent with loved ones to the dark moments of falling bombs, this is an honest account of a wartime child's formative years. Together with rare images and accounts from fellow evacuees who were sent to Cornwall to escape the ravages of war, this book reveals how these experiences are indelibly inscribed on the minds of wartime children.

978 0 7524 5540 2

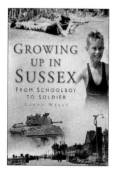

Growing Up in Sussex: From Schoolboy to Soldier
GERRY WELLS

This compelling memoir starts with a boy's journey through the early years of the 1930s – days of the rag and bone man, street lamplighters, Hercule Poirot, and in the background, Hitler. Then life gets real, at school where cane and cricket bat rule, where the mustard sandwich fills a hungry corner, and even more real with Army call-up, bullshit and training. In this nostalgic book evoking recollections of childhood and wartime in Sussex, the memories are the author's, however the sights and events are those that will be remembered by many others.

978 0 7524 4967 8

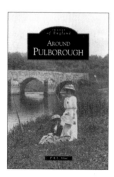

Around Pulborough
P.A.L. VINE

This fascinating collection of over 200 photographs explores Pulborough and its surrounding villages, including Hardham and Coldwatham to the south, Storrrington to the east, and Stopham, Fittleworth and Petworth to the west. The reader is taken on a tour of the area, from shops and businesses, greengrocers, fishmongers, saddlers and blacksmiths, to schools, houses and churches, and on to the water, where we meet the barge masters who navigated the waters transporting goods up and down between London, Arundel and Chichester.

978 0 7524 2611 2

Visit our website and discover thousands of other History Press books.

www.thehistorypress.co.uk